RESPONSIBLE KIDS:

6 Steps to Creating Them in an Irresponsible World

Judy Harmon Holmes, Ed.D.

Illustrated by Linda M. Brandt

WC Publishing

Copyright © 2021 Judy Ellen Harmon Holmes

All rights reserved. No part of this publication may be reproduced, distributed, or transmitted in any form or by any means, including photocopying, recording, digital scanning, or other electronic or mechanical methods, without the prior written consent of the publishers, except the case of brief quotations embodied in critical reviews and certain other non-commercial uses permitted by copyright law. For permission requests, please address WC Publishing.

ISBN: 978-0-9990489-5-5 (Paperback Edition)
ISBN: 978-0-9990489-6-2 (Kindle Edition)
ISBN: 978-0-999-0489-7-9 (eBook Edition)

Library of Congress Control Number 2021909960

Illustrations by Linda M. Brandt for Judy Harmon Holmes

Printed and bound in the United States of America

First printing August 2021

Published by WC Publishing
147 Patriot Lane
Elkton, Florida 32033-4058
Info@OnTargetWords.com

TABLE OF CONTENTS

BEFORE WE BEGIN   1

FIRST STEP
First Step to Creating *Irresponsible* Kids: Do Everything for Them   5
First Step to Creating *Responsible* Kids: Teach Them to Do It Themselves   7
TOOLS #1
Partial list of communication skills   29
The Communication/responsibility-blockers   30

SECOND STEP
Second Step to Creating *Irresponsible* Kids: Expect Nothing From Them   31
Second Step to Creating *Responsible* Kids: Teach Them to Take Part in Life Outside Themselves   33
TOOLS #2
Review & continuation of communication/responsibility-blockers   55
The missing information   56
More reasons to use the what question   60

THIRD STEP
Third Step to Creating *Irresponsible* Kids: Overlook Their Unacceptable Behavior   63
Third Step to Creating *Responsible* Kids: Teach Them to Deal with Uncomfortable Circumstances   65
TOOLS #3
Review of the I-message   82
Showing empathy by putting other's feelings into words   84
Showing interest and attention by paraphrasing   84
Essential process for using these three skills   85
The technique of providing choices   85
Making amends or restitution   86
Describing positive behavior and naming the trait we observed   87
Defining words in a chart   87

FOURTH STEP

FOURTH STEP TO CREATING *IRRESPONSIBLE* KIDS: FILL EVERY MOMENT FOR THEM — 89

FOURTH STEP TO CREATING *RESPONSIBLE* KIDS: TEACH THEM HOW TO MAKE HEALTHY CHOICES — 93

TOOLS # 4

REMINDERS FOR THE TEACHER — 105

NEW TOOLS IN THE FOURTH STEP TO CREATING RESPONSIBLE KIDS — 105

FIFTH STEP

FIFTH STEP TO CREATING *IRRESPONSIBLE* KIDS: SOLVE ALL THEIR PROBLEMS FOR THEM — 107

FIFTH STEP TO CREATING *RESPONSIBLE* KIDS: TEACH THEM HOW TO DEAL WITH DISAPPOINTMENT AND SOLVE PROBLEMS — 109

TOOLS #5

TWO NEW COMMUNICATION/RESPONSIBILITY BLOCKERS TO AVOID — 131

LIST OF COMMUNICATION/RESPONSIBILITY BLOCKERS — 131

COMMUNICATION/RESPONSIBILITY-BUILDING SKILLS THAT FOCUS AWAY FROM THE BLOCKERS — 132

GENTLE REMINDER ABOUT LISTENING TO THE LOUDER SPEAKER: FEELINGS OR WORDS — 132

PROBLEM-SOLVING — 132

SIXTH STEP

SIXTH STEP TO CREATING *IRRESPONSIBLE KIDS*: EXPECT OBEDIENCE — 135

SIXTH STEP TO CREATING *RESPONSIBLE* KIDS: TEACH THEM HOW TO WORK THROUGH A POWER STRUGGLE — 137

REFERENCE LIST — 153

ABOUT THE AUTHOR — 155

ENDNOTES — 157

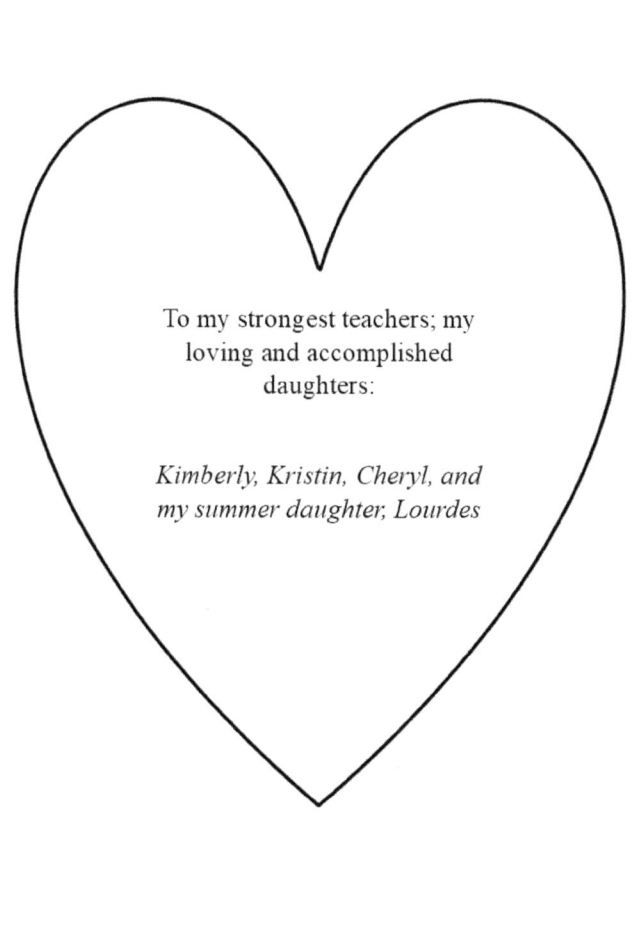

To my strongest teachers; my loving and accomplished daughters:

Kimberly, Kristin, Cheryl, and my summer daughter, Lourdes

ACKNOWLEDGEMENTS

There are many I would like to thank for their help and encouragement in writing this book, Warren Brewer for introducing the Karpman Drama Triangle to me; Stephen Karpman, MD for taking time to discuss his work with me; Fred Raskind for ongoing encouragement through the years; Beverly Eadie for being my first proofreader; my own children, grandchildren and all my students for providing diverse challenges and examples used in this book; and finally—Nancy at WC Publishing, my publisher, for making this book a reality.

Dear Reader,

As parents, we want what's best for our kids. We want them to be caring and dependable—to make good decisions, be trustworthy, do well in school, be productive team members, be respectful to adults and kind to their friends…in other words we want them to be responsible people.

We do the best job we know how, and the irony is that many of our actions—as well intended as they are—promote irresponsible behavior. Too often, and to our deep frustration and disappointment, we experience our children as sloppy, self-centered, lazy, rebellious, stubborn, and angry. Often, we find ourselves feeling discouraged and ready to give up.

Totally understandable because parenting is the hardest job we'll ever do. It's also the most important job we'll ever do. Here's the catch: parenting is the only job for which we have little or no training.

The purpose of this book is to show you, through many detailed examples, six effective steps to lead children and adolescents in learning *how* to become responsible and caring people. All learning is a process, so learning *how* to become responsible takes time. Each of the six steps requires you to spend a lot of time interacting with your children, and each way may challenge you to change the way you presently discipline.

The outcomes are worth it—a parent-child relationship that grows in love and respect, and children who become responsible, loving adults.

Today as I interact with my grown daughters' families and my beautiful eleven grandchildren, I am thankful I learned this process.

I think that you'll be glad you learned it, too–or at least–that is my heartfelt hope.

Do not give up!

Judy

Before We Begin

We have all seen the television ad showing the father and his young son sitting on the couch watching a game on TV. The father drinks from a bottle of soda and his son does the same, even taking his sip at the same time as his dad. Then we see an alternate scenario. The father is drinking a bottle of water, and the son too is drinking a bottle of water, still taking his sip at the same time as his dad.

These ads show the strong impact of modeling on children's behavior. Every recommendation in this book is based on the premise that what we model as parents is what our children will also do. What we say, how we say it, and what we do models for our children how to talk and how to behave. In other words, parents are continuously modeling how to live life.

Several years ago, I visited a kindergarten during "play time" (no longer a part of the curriculum). Two little girls were pretending to be mommies, and as I listened and watched, I had a bird's eye view into their homes. One little girl was incredibly angry with her "child." The kindergartener wrinkled her forehead, and with a hand squeezing each shoulder of her doll, yelled, "You're a bad girl. If you don't stop crying, you're going to bed right after dinner." As they continued to play, I overheard the other say to her "crying" doll, "Honey, I know you want that piece of candy and it's hard to wait. It's time for dinner right now, and after that you can have the candy."

Just listening to this short exchange, I could hear a world of difference in the parenting of each of these children. In our culture most of us know only two ways to parent; strict or lenient. There is, however, a third model, one I refer to as "lead parenting," based on Dr. William Glasser's "lead teacher"[1] method. When parents discipline through a lead parenting model, they engage their children in processes that teach children *how* to become responsible for their words and their actions.

Parents who are leaders rather than either of the extremes of lenient or strict, model and engage their children in processes for how to carry out daily responsibilities, how to take an active part in life outside themselves, how to have a discussion about issues, how to make healthy choices in their activities, how to deal with disappointment and solve problems, how to live with consequences of their decisions, and how to work through power struggles instead of fighting.

Very few of us had a role model of Lead Parenting, so the process for becoming one feels unnatural and uncomfortable at first. It certainly was for me. I was raised by a most lenient parent and my husband by an extremely strict parent. Needless to say, our parenting models clashed and usually we ended up capriciously using both models with no consistency. We didn't know of any alternatives, and we wanted our children to be responsible people who cared about others and appreciated what they had. We certainly didn't want them to be "spoiled."

Most of the time, my husband and I settled into being strict parents. We made "reasonable" rules and held our children to these rules. If they disobeyed the rules, we gave them a "reasonable" punishment. Most of our friends were parenting the same way and our children seemed to be doing just fine. Oh sure, we had power struggles over the usual things: putting away their toys, picking up their rooms, bedtime curfew, feeding the dog; just the usual. We felt confident with our strict parenting which I call "Boss parent," based on Glasser's "Boss teacher."[2]

When our youngest entered kindergarten, I started teaching high school English, and needless to say, I was a Boss teacher. This too was working fine; at least I believed it was. A couple of years into my teaching career, I enrolled in a Masters' Program in School Counseling. Immediately, I was introduced to an alternative model for parenting; the parent as leader and guide instead of boss, or, as developmental psychologist Diana Baumrind called this kind of parent in her research, the Authoritative Parent.[3]

I learned that parents don't have to be either lenient or strict; in fact, I learned that by adolescence, children of parents who consistently use the skills of Authoritative Parenting were, in comparison to their peers, more "…mature, resilient, optimistic, and perceived their parents as loving and influential…. They were self-regulated and socially responsible and had high self-esteem….” In addition, studies showed that children of Authoritative Parents tend to earn higher math and verbal scores on achievement tests than those of children with strict or lenient parents. Weren't all these things just what my husband and I wanted for our own children?

We started taking parenting courses together, and we learned how to become authoritative instead of authoritarian. We learned that authoritative, or as I call it, lead parents, are parents who combine firm rules and consequences along with warmth and nurturing. Becoming lead parents required us to learn new skills for working with our children. It was definitely not easy, but despite the struggles, we experienced many encouragements that showed us the success of modeling the lead parent discipline path. One such indication of success occurred as I was teaching a sophomore English class how to problem-solve differences when they worked together in groups. Specifically, I was teaching them to use the language of responsibility, also known as relationship-building communication skills.

A student raised her hand and asked if Cheryl Holmes, a senior at a different high school, were my daughter. When I said yes, she went on to say that Cheryl was training her to be a waitress at the local pizza shop and that she talked the way I was teaching them to talk. Then she added, "When I work with her, she doesn't make me feel stupid when I make mistakes."

Today I observe that my now adult children are incorporating these skills into their relationship with their own children, and I'm already observing my grandchildren using these interpersonal skills. Relearning is never easy, but based on my personal experience, as well as on the research, I can say emphatically that the ongoing results of becoming a lead parent are worth the struggle.

And witnessing the results two generations later is truly one of the most rewarding experiences of my life.

It's really important to understand what's going on with us human beings. It's called a power struggle. Power struggles are inevitable in life–our first five chapters are filled with examples. Our culture, for-the-most-part, teaches us to respond to a power struggle in one of two ways:

1. **Fighting**–ordering, demanding, name-calling, shaming, and, yes, yelling louder than the other guy, or any of the other responsibility/communication-stopper tactics we had learned by the time we were talking
2. **Suppression**–holding the anger inside and walking away, or just crying

Fight or flight is a survival mechanism programed into all of us. But most of our interactions do not require either response–we've just learned those along the way as we watch and listen to others interact. There are alternatives and we'll look at those along the way in the next chapters.

And yes, the alternatives do allow us to stick up for ourselves within this process. So, are you ready to learn some new tools for effective communication with your kids–and everyone else?

Let's get started on learning this process.

STEP 1

FIRST STEP TO CREATING *IRRESPONSIBLE* KIDS

Do Everything *for Them*

It's easier to do it yourself and you're so tired of reminding and nagging them:

"Hang up your coat."
"Did you feed the dog?"
"Make your bed before you leave."

And then what do you get but responses that range from totally ignoring you: "Yeah, okay," said by your seven-year-old as she stares hypnotically at the television, to theatrics from your thirteen-year-old who screams, "How come you never say anything to Megan? Her room's always a mess."

And homework? Kids almost always wait until the last minute and then rush through it. Then one of you ends up doing most of it so they won't get a bad grade. Who has time for this? And who needs the stress?

So, you have learned to save a great deal of hassle if you just do it yourself. If your child is very young, say around two, you pick up their toys. If you have older children, around seven and ten, you make their beds for them. You hang up the clothes they left strewn over the floor, *and* you are still putting away those toys. You're no doubt continuing to wake up your sixth grader for school every day, and yes, still nagging everyone to eat their breakfasts and to "hurry up or you'll miss your bus."

Then, as the bus pulls away with your children actually on it, you discover the forgotten lunch money or gym clothes or book bag, and as you dash out the door to get to your own job, you grab the forgotten item and drop it off at school, all the while realizing you are–yet again–late yourself. Kids! Will they ever learn to be responsible?

And the answer is "No."

At least not all by themselves.

FIRST STEP TO CREATING *RESPONSIBLE* KIDS

Teach Them How to Do It Themselves

When we parents don't allow our children to experience the consequences of their behavior, we take away their need to *become* responsible. Boss and Pushover Parents do not allow their children to experience the results of their behavior.

Lead Parents allow their children to experience any uncomfortable outcomes of irresponsible behavior while at the same time guiding them through the process and teaching them how to make responsible choices the next time. When we change our own behavior, we provide the opportunity for our children to learn how to become responsible.

Sounds simple, but contrary to what many people believe, parenting is teaching, and *teaching* is not merely telling and explaining. Teaching is a *process*, and teachers call that process a lesson plan.

1. Create a Learning Goal for the Behavior You Expect Your Child to Know and Be Able to Do

Sit down with your child and explain the learning goal. Include reasons it is important to do this without your help.

2. Plan the Activity for Practicing and for Carrying Out the Learning Goal

Give Information but avoid "lecturing." Working together, put the learning goal into words and then brainstorm some ways to go about accomplishing it. Describe in detail what you will be doing and will not be doing to help with the learning. Decide on a plan. Perhaps it's to buy an alarm clock (because it is a novelty for today's kids) and first, let your child practice getting herself up. After a couple mornings, the expectation is that she gets herself up and ready without reminders.

> "It's important to be on time for school, so we're going to make a plan for how you can do that on your own. When you miss the school bus, and we take you to school, we end up being late for our jobs. We can't do that anymore."
> *Or,*
> "We can't ask Mrs. Mack to take you to school because it interrupts her plans for the morning."
> (*Or whatever the reasons may be.*)

3. Establish Consequences and Carry Through on Them

Together, discuss consequences and how they are connected to the choices we make. Give some examples and discuss the ways privileges and responsibilities go together. Brainstorm developmentally-appropriate natural and/or logical consequences that can/might result if children/adolescents don't carry out their responsibilities. Explain that they get to "practice" a new task for a week or so, and after that you expect them to be responsible for that task until it's changed.

- A *Natural Consequence* is something that would "naturally" occur because of the person's behavior. An example might be

getting a zero on a test if the student wasn't in class and had an unexcused lateness or absence.
- A *Logical Consequence* is something that would be a "logical" result of the person's behavior. An example might be having to go to bed earlier to be able to get up on time. Parents, or parents *and* child, can create the consequences to match the behavior.

4. Demonstrate and Model the Expected Behavior in Your Own Actions

Psychologists have known for many years that *Modeling* behaviors is one of the strongest teaching strategies known. Demonstrating how to act and how to take responsibility–especially when we're angry–will usually create the greatest challenge for parents because it includes the ways we talk and act with everyone:
- our child's Lacrosse coach
- the rude grocery store cashier
- the unreasonable teacher
- that obnoxious driver
- and–most importantly–the way we model talking to one another in our homes

This is usually a huge learning goal for us.

5. Guide, Encourage, Observe, and Listen as They Practice

Yes, "Practice." The change in behavior won't happen overnight. Every behavior needs to be practiced. Doing something new is hard work for all of us. As your children practice, give encouragement:

Tell them you recognize how hard the work is:
- "It's really hard to get up so early."
- "I wish we could all sleep in."

Tell them you recognize what they've been successful at so far:

- "We've noticed that since you've been packing your book bag the night before, you've had everything ready when the bus comes."

Show empathy for them and avoid criticizing and reminding them when they make mistakes and must live with the consequences:
- "We wish you didn't have to go to bed an hour earlier to get enough sleep. If getting more sleep leads to success in being on time, next week we can try the original plan again."

Throughout the whole process, observe and listen to learn each child's frustration points as well as specific ways to help each different child achieve success. Every child is unique and it's important to **observe** and **listen** carefully to each child in the family.

6. Repeat This Process as Often as It Takes, Never Giving Up

This is a discipline that teaches kids how to become responsible: giving information, demonstrating/modeling, creating an activity for them to practice the task, guiding, and encouraging, observing, and listening—repeating as often as it takes and never giving up.

Examples

Staying with that oh-so-familiar issue of the morning hassle of getting our kids up and out the door every morning, let's look at how the scene typically goes, and then see how we might apply our Lesson Plan:

> **The Morning Scramble**
>
> "Steve, Sam, Time to get up."
> *(You hurry back to getting yourself dressed for work, and about five minutes later realize you've heard no movement from the bedroom.)*
> "Come on boys. You've got thirty minutes before the bus comes."
> No response
> *(You go in and shake them gently, pulling off the covers.)*
> "Boys, you have to have time for breakfast."
> *(You vaguely feel your jaw tightening.)*
> "Yeah, yeah, I'll be right there," Steve mumbles as he pulls the sheet back up and over his head.
> "Get up right this minute!"
> *(And now you know your jaw is aching.)*

By the time they do get up–with your constant reminders–and have gathered all their school stuff (you hope), you end up frazzled and driving them to school again. And there you are thinking, "When will they learn to be responsible?"

And, of course, the answer is, "It will not happen as long as we parents are carrying out the responsibilities that belong to our kids."

Okay, let's see the plan in action. You and the boys have completed the plan together, and everyone is ready to begin.

The Learning Goal might look like this:

Steve and Sam will get up for school when their alarm rings. They'll get dressed, brush teeth, eat breakfast, have all needed school supplies ready, and be on time to catch the school bus. Dad and Mom may give a reminder once a morning during the **first** week and then **no more** reminders."

"Yeah, right!" you're thinking. "In my dreams."

Well, the fact is, because Steve and Sam are *developmentally* ready to learn how to do this series of tasks, we need to teach them *how* to take on this responsibility. Remembering that teaching is not merely telling and explaining but rather a series of tasks in a planned process, we begin the lesson.

It's always productive to post the learning goal in plain sight– maybe on the refrigerator. During the first couple of days, you can review it with your children, and ask if they have any questions.

For the activity itself, you might start by giving each child the gift of his very own alarm clock. Yes, I know a cell phone has an alarm, but an alarm clock is "dramatic" and more likely to get their attention. Now your kids probably haven't asked for one, will find it strange, and may well retort with, "And I want this clock WHY?"

This is your segue to emphasize that this activity really is happening. Most families are great at starting, but weak at carry through. Give more information.

"Well, guys, we think the alarm clock is louder, and we know you hate it when we nag and nag to get you up. We agreed that we would give you a wakeup call just once each morning during the first week– and the first week only. We think the alarm clock can help us stay off your backs."

You have now just repeated the parameters or boundaries of the learning activity.

At this point most parents are feeling, at best, pessimistically hopeful. "What if he just sleeps through, misses the bus, and I end up having to take him to school?"

During the first week, this may happen, but whatever you established as the age-appropriate natural and logical consequence must *also* happen.

Perhaps the consequence is that bedtime will have to be earlier because the child is obviously too tired to get up in the morning (which may be the case). Perhaps it's that he walks to school (if age-appropriate) and you can always follow invisibly behind for safety. In my experience, children dislike both consequences and will work to avoid them, especially if they have experienced them once or twice.

Now most parents have a deep reluctance to allow their children to experience the natural and logical consequences of their behavior. They would rather take away an Xbox or ground the child than have them experience the natural consequences. There's something really scary about natural consequences. They're so REAL. But remember, you are teaching, so you are still guiding, and, as any effective teacher knows, are now allowing your child to learn from the outcomes of his or her decisions.

Let's say the consequence you agreed upon is to walk to school. Further, say this walk is a few miles. How many times will kids repeat oversleeping when the natural consequences of their mistake are uncomfortable? And if you happen to live where it's cold in the winter? Speeds up the learning!

~ ~ ~ ~

A wonderful example of this situation occurred with Keith, a ninth-grade boy in my first period English class. The third time he came wandering into class late, I called his mom to let her know how his lateness was affecting his work. We decided to meet, and the three of us sat down to discuss the problem. She described the tense mornings trying to get him out of bed and onto the bus.

He admitted he ignored her until the very last possible moment, and "besides," he continued, "what difference does it make anyway? My mom always drives me to school, and I get to sleep an extra half hour."

"Do you enjoy your mother's nagging every morning?" I asked.

Slender shoulders hunched in a kind of so-what shrug.

"Would you like it if your parents stopped treating you like a little kid?"

"Well, yeah," he said in a "well, duh" tone.

"What are some things you might do to help them start treating you as more grown up?" I asked because asking a "what" question puts the responsibility on *him*.

He hesitated, and then he looked at me. "You mean like not being late for school?"

"That's one way," I responded. "Do you think if you got yourself to school on time, your parents might see you taking responsibility for yourself, and start to see you as growing up?"

He looked at his mother. She smiled and nodded.

I gave information, included the parameters about getting and using the alarm clock and asked Mom to guide and support by reminding him, if needed, once each morning after the alarm rang. This reminder would only be for the first week. Both agreed. Then I dropped the bombshell.

"You know, Keith, this means if you don't get up, you walk to school."

"Oh, I couldn't let him walk!" Mom blurted out. "It's five miles from our house."

I suggested he could call her a couple of times from his cell phone as he walked. With massive misgivings, she agreed, and Keith did too, though not enthusiastically.

That evening Keith's mom called me at home. "I've been thinking about this whole thing, and I can't let him walk all that way. It's winter. What kind of mother would I be?"

"The best kind," I replied, "because you're teaching him how to be responsible at a time when you're there to guide and support him as he's learning."

I continued to reassure her with the suggestion that if the cell didn't give her enough confidence, she could get in her car and follow invisibly behind.

"Besides," I added, "how many times do you think he'll want to take this walk?"

And for Keith, it took two walks before he decided to take on his responsibility to get to school on time. He wasn't late again that year. Mom did drive "invisibly" behind, and he never knew she was right there protecting him.

~ ~ ~ ~

Parents ask, "What if you live next door to the school?" One option for a natural consequence is to let your son or daughter live with the consequences meted out by the school—a detention, a lower grade for missing the opening work, etc.—whatever the school has in place.

But too often school consequences are ineffective because they're carried out several days or longer after the incident. For consequences to be most effective, they must follow the incident right away. In such situations, parents can opt for *logical* consequences. Then, remembering that *privileges and responsibilities are partners*, take away or limit a privilege of value to the child until they show they can take the responsibility of getting to school on time.

As for forgotten items like lunch money, book bags, etc., let the natural consequences happen. This lesson is usually harder for parents than it is for children. Go back to the learning objective for a reminder of why this objective is important. It makes more sense to let children go without lunch one or two days, or suffer a detention for not having gym clothes, or even get a lower grade in a class–at a time in their lives when parents and teachers are consistently present to guide, support, and encourage, them.

The object is to prevent their having to grow up in a nagging, negative atmosphere and suffer the much harder consequences of irresponsible behavior when they have a job or college classes–and there's no one there to teach them a responsible way to behave.

The effective teacher does not solve the problems, but rather, creates the learning objective for a necessary lesson, gives information *including* the boundaries, demonstrates the desired objective, creates learning activities for the student to practice, and then guides, and gives encouragement. During all of this, the teachers are listening and observing to learn about the students in order to increase effective teaching. Remember, parents *are* teachers!

Even the best students don't always follow the teacher's suggestions and parameters. For example, some may choose not to do their assigned reading and end up failing a quiz or an exam. Ineffective teachers give constant reminders. They nag or lecture on the dire results of irresponsibility.

The effective teachers know the difficult art of stepping back and allowing students to struggle for a short time–even to the point of failure if necessary–but they never give up on that student!

Even though they have stepped back, the effective teacher/parent continues to offer additional information, to offer help in creating a plan for success, and to offer additional practice activities–all the while being certain to not do the work for the students nor to rescue them from the natural consequences of their decisions.

Parents have many opportunities to teach their children how to do things for themselves. When we resist the tendency to do everything for our children, and instead, guide them in learning how to do things themselves, they learn how to become responsible. When our elementary child gets a low grade on a test and doesn't understand what he did wrong, we can encourage him to go to the teacher on his own, and hopefully we've been modeling parent-teacher-child meetings since he started school.

When your middle schooler needs a dentist appointment, you can help her make the appointment herself, gradually giving the job entirely to her. When we take a child with us to the grocery store, we can model reading the labels as we discuss why we're doing that, and gradually turn over some of the grocery shopping to our teen who just got her driver's license. When we create our budget for the month and pay our bills, we can involve our children. The list of ways to guide our children in learning how to become responsible is endless.

Parents ask, "When should I begin teaching my child to become responsible? What is the best age?" Ideally, we begin the teaching with little "pre-lessons" when our children are bitsies. We talk to them as we do our daily activities: washing dishes, making the bed, going shopping etc., telling them what we are doing and why. When we explain why we're doing a task, we're helping our children make connections and see the relationships among tasks and decisions, thus helping them to begin learning how life functions–how things "fit" together.

One idea for helping bitsies learn about taking responsibility is to encourage them to "help." As you put away your one-and-a-half-year old's clothes, give her information by telling her what you're doing and why you are doing it. At this age kids love to help–for a minute or two–and when she does, guide her by assisting as she attempts the task, encourage her by telling her how neatly she folded the washcloth or her sock, or how helpful it is that she put her shirt into the drawer–even if later, you return to sort things out.

The point is you are laying the foundation for him to develop responsibility by giving information (Step 1 of the plan), modeling the task (Step 4), guiding him as he begins to practice (Step 5), and encouraging him throughout (Step 5). The point with littles is to have them participate in a needed activity and have fun doing it.

Through these shared learning activities, our children are not the only ones learning. As we observe and listen, we're learning how our child learns, how long she's able to stay with a task, as well as the ways in which she shows she's bored or frustrated. In other words, we are learning how to be the best possible parent for *this* particular child.

An appropriate way to involve littles is helping them pick up toys. Following the lesson plan process, here's a possible scenario with a two-year-old. Please notice that the steps in the lesson plan below are abbreviated a bit to meet the developmental needs of a two-year-old. It's not practical to structure a formal learning goal or consequences with children under two and a half.

~ ~ ~ ~

1. *Giving information*: Tell her it's time to put things away, adding a reason she can understand. "It's time to put your toys away so we can eat our lunch." You set the parameters by showing her the toy box where the toys go.
2. *Creating activities for "students" to practice learning how to do the task and to solve the problem*: "Let's play a game. I'll put in a toy and then you take a turn."
3. *Demonstrating/Modeling*: You toss a toy into the toy box.
4. *Guiding, Encouraging, Observing, and Listening* to learn everything possible about how she learns and how she becomes frustrated. Work alongside your child until she's ready to do it on her own. Maybe at first, she just stands there staring. You can Encourage by saying something like, "What do you think?" If she doesn't respond, you might say, "Come on, it's your turn." If needed, you can always add, "Let's see who can pick up the most toys." As you work-play together, be putting her strengths into words. "I'll bet you can lift that truck right up off the floor and put it in the box."

5. *Repeating Everything as Often as It Takes/Never Giving Up*: If your child loses interest before the toys are all taken care of, you can point out what he accomplished. "Look, you put away six toys, good job." Then the two of you walk away, leaving the rest where they are.

Now, you may be thinking, "But, isn't this teaching him he doesn't have to finish the job?"

Remember, each step in the lesson plan is relevant to the developmental stage of our child. In actuality, you have just provided the atmosphere for him to remember the fun he had picking up his toys. He's just beginning to learn and so are *you*.

You have learned especially important information about your child's frustration tolerance–information that will help you to be a more effective and loving parent. There may have been too many toys for him to handle, or if he got cranky, perhaps he was tired or hungry. So next time, you alter the activity part of the plan by giving him fewer toys at a time and playing the "put away" game whenever new toys are needed or by starting the cleanup a bit earlier before he's tired or hungry. You decide based on what you learn about your child.

This is Lead Teaching–and Lead Parenting. It is vastly different from Boss Parenting which will result in the child refusing to comply either in a meltdown or a temper tantrum. The power struggle scene is avoided, and you've accomplished the lesson that your bitsy can absorb and learn–in love and peace.

~ ~ ~ ~

While each of these steps is of paramount importance, the last one bears examining more deeply. "How often and for how long do we have to go through all these steps?" The long answer is "always," and "forever." And to top it all off, the older our children become, the more difficult–and important–the lessons become. This means too, the lessons get harder and harder to teach.

Let's take a minute and look again at the profession of teaching. When we know that the percentage of teachers who leave the field within the first five years is as high as seventeen percent (almost 1/5) on average[4], we gain a little perspective on the difficulty of teaching. And these teachers had at least four years of study and an extensive internship to prepare them! Parents have little or no training for being a parent, and parenting is the most important job we'll ever do.

Whether or not the students continue to do their learning tasks, the effective teacher or parent continues to give guidance, support, and encouragement, especially at those times when the children, despite the adult's efforts, may have made irresponsible choices and consequently must accept and live with the natural consequences.

By now it's probably noticeably clear that being Lead Parents who are teaching their children how to do things for themselves is not easy, and this is only Step One in teaching them how to become responsible! Teaching responsibility is a process that is not only time consuming and difficult, but also often more painful for the parents than for the children. This is particularly the case when we have to step back and allow our children to struggle, to make mistakes, and to live with the consequences, while we remain on the side with support and guidance, never giving up.

In the classroom we call this being "the guide on the side" instead of the "sage on the stage."

~ ~ ~ ~

At this point, parents usually comment "Okay, so we understand that we're supposed to give lots of encouragement, express empathy and understanding for how hard the lesson is, and guide and support while we stand back and let our kids live with the natural or logical consequences of their behavior. But frankly, when is enough, *enough*? When do we give our kids a well-deserved punishment?"

If this is one of your questions, please go online and look up the effects of punishment on children. Note particularly the differences in outcomes between children who are *punished* for their misbehavior versus children who are *guided and supported* as they live with the natural or logical consequences of misbehavior. Which of these alternatives has the stronger results in teaching children how to become responsible for their own behavior? For now, just do this much research and the subject will definitely come up again in this book.

Let's examine the reactions of our children to this process of carrying out a lesson plan. In the beginning, most kids think it's a great way to get their parents off their back, but sooner or later, you'll be hearing such statements as "This is stupid!" and "None of my friends' parents make them do this stupid stuff." And sometimes, even, "I am not doing this anymore. I'll just sleep until you wake me up." Usually followed by a stomping off–behavior which for most parents, has the same effect as waving a red flag at a bull.

Caution: The usual comebacks don't model and teach our kids how to become responsible, but they certainly escalate things to a lose-lose situation and pretty quickly. We get angry and typically shoot back with something like any of the following "Roadblocks to Communication" identified and classified by Dr. Thomas Gordon[5].

Ordering	"Don't be so disrespectful."
Warning	"Keep that kind of talk up and you'll be grounded."
Sarcasm	"You're always on time when it's something YOU want to do."
Criticizing	"You're just being lazy."
Lecturing	"This is not showing responsibility. A responsible person would have called us to let us know ____."
Nagging	"Come on. I've told you three times already!"
Giving advice	"What you need to do is ____."

With each of these retorts, we have changed the subject from meeting our learning goal to something else—disrespect, laziness, etc.

If these are indeed issues, then they need to be addressed later. Right now, we have to stick to the subject of the learning goal.

So, instead of changing the subject, we restrain ourselves, and we model a response that promotes responsibility in our children. First, we put *their* feelings into words.[6] Ask yourself, "what is the emotion behind my child's angry words?" Then we say something that states those feelings. We might say, "I know you're feeling very frustrated/discouraged/etc. with this process." Or "I know this isn't easy for you."

Why in the world would we do that? Doesn't such a response signal that it's okay to show disrespect?

Not at all, because empathic responses keep everyone on the topic of the learning goal and keep the responsibility for meeting that goal right where it belongs–on the child. We haven't gotten onto other topics such as rudeness and self-centeredness. We will be addressing the rudeness issue, but not now because we need to address one issue at a time.

When I started responding to my children by verbalizing *their* feelings instead of using my usual responses from the list above, I found the process very difficult. I felt artificial, stilted, and totally uncomfortable. Then, in the heat of an altercation, I could not remember what to say and that threw me even more off balance. To help me remember, I chose two statements to memorize so I had them ready. It helped somewhat, but the constant practice my girls provided for me was the best help.

The surprising outcome my husband and I experienced was the reaction of our children to these nonjudgmental responses to their anger. We found the typical response was anything from a puzzled look to a "Whatever!" And then, they usually went back to working on the learning goal even if they were grumpy about it.

On occasion, I'd hear "Yeah, and I'm not doing it." At that point parents have to let it go because the process of the plan *will* continue, and the consequences for "not doing it" are in place along with our continued guidance and support.

Later, when tempers have calmed down, it's time for us to have a little talk with our children to teach them–or review and reteach them–how to handle their anger and frustration in a responsible, respectful way.

This same process of the lesson goal and plan continues as we teach our children how to become responsible in other usually problematic areas of life: riding in the car and not fighting (with sibling), going shopping and accepting "no," doing homework on time, feeding the dog regularly, sharing with others graciously, etc., etc.

We create the activity–the real-life activity–give information, allow for practice with guidance, model the behavior ourselves, provide ongoing support, hold our children to the consequences established, and repeat the process over and over for as long as it takes–all the while avoiding the Roadblocks to Communication.

Will our kids ever learn to be responsible? Yes, but only if we change our *own* behavior to guide and support them as they experience a process for learning how to become responsible.

Sample Scenarios

Below are examples of a parent *using* these skills in difficult, but typical types of conversations between a parent and child. You may find them helpful *and* familiar.

The Honeymoon is Over

One way to have a productive discussion when the task has lost its novelty–usually sometime into the second week of a new activity–is demonstrated below by a parent and their 5th grader.

> **Child**: "I *hate* this stupid 'activity.'"
> **Parent**: "I know it's really hard work to keep doing this day after day." *(The parent puts child's feelings into words.)*

Child: "No, it's NOT hard! It's STUPID, I told you." (*The child may be screaming at this point.*)
Parent: "What do you think might work better?"
(*Parent uses the "what" question format.*)
Child: "Just let me sleep in and then you can take me to school if I miss the bus. That's what you've always done before."
Parent: "When I drive you to school, I end up late for work and I can't do that."
(*Parent provides information that was probably discussed in the initial planning discussion **without** a lecture. You'll repeat this many times over the weeks and months it takes to learn. Stay calm. Don't give up.*)
Child: "So? What difference does it make? You're the boss. You can go in any time you want."
Parent: "Actually, I can't. Others are waiting for me and they depend on me to do my part in our work." (*Gives information about parent's responsibility to others and models its importance.*)
Child: "So what? It's *your* business. You can just tell them to start without you, and then you can take me to school. COME ON; I hate this whole stupid thing you're making me do." (*This may be the start of a meltdown.*)
Parent: "I know you hate it, Honey, and you believe it's stupid. We believe it's very important for you to learn how to take on this responsibility for yourself. You know

what I've noticed? I've noticed that both Wednesday and Thursday, you got yourself up, ready, ate breakfast, and were on the bus with all your stuff, *and* nobody reminded you even once." (*Puts child's feelings into words and repeats the object without lecturing. Gives encouragement by noting successes.*)

Child: "Yeah, but I don't want to do it anymore. Maybe I just *won't* do it."

Parent: "You can make that decision, but do you think it's a good choice?"

Child: "What do you mean?"

Parent: "What happens if you miss the bus?" (*Uses a what question to encourage the child to think about the consequences they've agreed on, no threats.*)

Child: "You mean I have to walk all the way to school? I'll *really* be late then!" (*If this is not appropriate for your situation, think of a logical consequence for this lesson.*)

Parent: *Remains silent, employing "wait time.*[7]*"*

Child: "Whatever! This is so STUPID!"

Notice that in this conversation, the parent is only using statements that keep the responsibility on the child. The child is free to choose, but s/he knows s/he will have to live with the consequences.

A Conversation About Handling Angry and Rude Outbursts

A parent has asked a child (any age from 8 or 9–sometimes younger–to adolescent) to sit down at an agreed upon time and discuss an earlier outburst. The child comes into the room and slams himself into a chair with obvious "attitude."

Parent: "I know when I'm angry, it's very hard for me to talk calmly and I know you're having the same struggle."
(Silence. Allows Wait Time.)
Child: "Well, if you're *so* 'understanding' then you *understand* why I yelled at you and walked out on what you were saying. You were being so unfair!"
Parent: *(Does not react to the sarcasm.)* "I do understand your feeling of wanting to lash out and I understand that you were very angry."
Child: "Then, what's the big deal? Everyone gets mad."
Parent: (*Employs the "what" question.*) "Yes, everyone gets mad. Here's a question for you. What are some ways you might have handled your anger in a better way–a way that could help you instead of getting you in trouble?"
Child: "I don't want to talk about it. This is so dumb."
(Wait time. If child continues not to talk, parent can offer an idea.)
Parent: (*Child may not be agreeable to anything right now. Try anyway.*) "I can give you one idea if you'd like."
Child: (*Still has an attitude but reluctantly agrees.*) "Whatever. Go ahead."
Parent: "One thing you might do is *say* how you're feeling, something like, 'I'm

> really mad right now.' Then *ask* for what you want, maybe, 'Can we talk about this when I get my anger under control?'"
> *(Silence as child glares at the floor. Allow Wait Time.)*
>
> **Note**: *Your child may or may not agree, may or may not continue saying that the whole discussion is stupid. You, meanwhile, are observing and listening to learn more about your child's frustration levels and skills for handling their frustration. If you find that you need to be more direct, you may begin or continue the conversation with something like the following:*
>
> **Parent**: (*Use an I-Message–describe behavior, describe your feelings in relation to the behavior, and state what you expect. This method avoids blame and criticism*).[8]
> "I know you're angry. So am I. This is very important to discuss, and when you yell at me (*swear, storm off, etc.*), I get even angrier. I expect us both to be respectful to each other no matter what the situation."

Employ *Wait Time*. If your child says nothing, you might continue with the *What* question, "What are some ways we can do that?" Then as the discussion continues, you continue to avoid the Roadblocks to Communication and instead use communication that promotes responsibility.

If your child refuses to engage, or if she continues to scream things like, "You just don't understand," or "Don't you remember what it was like when you were my age?" or any of the other out-of-control-things many kids say, then she's refusing to take responsibility for her anger and her behavior. You, though, continue to model respect and self-control.

When this happens, there are consequences. If she's unwilling to take responsibility for her behavior, then she is unable to take responsibility for mature privileges like having a cell phone, for instance. With *every* privilege comes responsibility. A logical consequence might be for a parent to take the cell phone or other important item away until the child has shown they are able to do as expected. This is usually just a couple of days the first time.

Just know that when you do this, the irresponsible behavior will probably escalate, and you will be on the edge of losing it with her and using *all* the responsibility-blocking statements. In fact, you probably will slip and use one or two–totally normal reaction. Hang in there though and employ your preplanned responsibility-building statement.

Then end the interchange with something like, "When you have your anger under control, please let me know, and we can continue our conversation."

You end it at this point. You have given her the responsibility to continue the conversation with you when she's calmed down.

Helping children, especially adolescents, learn to handle their emotions in responsible ways is incredibly challenging and takes a great deal of time. However, it's perhaps the most important skill set we can teach them.

TOOLS #1

Partial List of Communication Skills That Promote Responsibility (and help to build and maintain loving relationships)

1. Show empathy by putting the other's feelings into words
2. Giving brief information/reasons
3. Modeling what you want your children to know and do
4. Modeling how you want your child to use these skills
5. Giving encouragement by describing what the child has accomplished so far
6. Describing behavior without judgment, blame, or conclusions
7. Giving "wait time" (originally for teachers, but great for parents too)
8. Asking a "What" question
9. All the while, holding your own frustration at your child's rudeness for a later discussion (which will take place)
10. Using an I-Message[9] (Avoids beginning with "you" because "you" feels accusatory. It also leads to the trap of using communication/relationship blockers. See examples in the preceding sample scenarios)
11. Holding the line on the natural and/or logical consequences already in place

The Communication/Responsibility-Blockers
(that promote negativity in relationships)

1. Ordering
2. Warning
3. Using Sarcasm
4. Criticizing/Judging
5. Lecturing
6. Reminding/Nagging
7. Giving Advice/Solving the Problem for the Child
8. Asking the "Why Question"

STEP 2

SECOND STEP TO CREATING *IRRESPONSIBLE* KIDS

Expect Nothing *from Them*

After all, they work hard in school all day and then they have sports practices and music lessons. And there's homework every day. Their games are every weekend. And of course, it's important for them to have friends and fun. They're only children for a short period of time.

They are so busy with all these activities as it is that they're lucky if they get into bed by 9:30 or later. That's the reality of life, and it's just not fair to expect them to do anything more.

I even feel guilty when I ask them to help around the house because their schedule is so full already, and besides, they just forget. Reminding them all the time exhausts me and we end up fighting. It's just not worth the aggravation.

And I really need their teachers to understand how much they have to do and cut them some slack when they have to turn work in late or when they're just having a bad day. They're already under more stress than ever before.

They're only kids! These are supposed to be the most carefree days of their lives, and they should be able to enjoy all of it.

SECOND STEP TO CREATING *RESPONSIBLE* KIDS

Teach Them How *to Take Part in Life* Outside *Themselves*

Looking back at the preceding parental concerns, we see that everything is about the children; the children's schedules, the children's activities, the children's interests. While this situation may be the reality of our children's world today, it isn't the reality of life.

If we want to teach our children how to become responsible, our job is not only teaching them how to become responsible for their own words and actions, but also how to become responsible for contributing to family needs and for being a contributing member of a group.

When we enable our kids to think and act only on behalf of their own needs and interests as we hover nearby, we're teaching them to become self-centered and, in all too many cases, callous of others' needs and interests.

Here's a common child expectation:

> **The Soccer Uniform**
>
> **Adolescent**: "Where's my soccer uniform?"
>
> **Mom**: "Isn't it in your closet?"
>
> **Adolescent**: "No! *You* were supposed to wash it. You *knew* I had a game today."
>
> **Mom**: "I'm sorry, Honey. Where did you put it?"
>
> **Adolescent**: (*Impatience obvious*) "I left it in my room. You could have checked!"
>
> **Mom**: (*Anger obvious*) "And *you* should have put it in the laundry. Had you done that; you'd have a clean uniform."

Now the stage is set for a power struggle, and the real issue of the dirty uniform will be forgotten as both mother and daughter blame each other.

Let's alter this scenario just enough to show what might transpire when the parent has taught the child that they have an age-appropriate responsibility for taking care of their personal belongings–and then consistently has held the child to that expectation. Notice the implication for responsibility in the "What" question.

> **Adolescent**: "Where's my soccer uniform?"
>
> **Mom**: "Isn't it in your closet? I didn't see it in the laundry."
>
> **Adolescent**: (Runs to check bedroom) "Oh no, I forgot to put it in the laundry."
>
> **Mom**: I'm sorry, Honey. What are you going to do?"
>
> **Adolescent**: "I'll check to see if my other uniform is clean. If it isn't, I'll have to sit on the bench and not play. (*Child is angry/frustrated*.) That's such a stupid rule."

In the second scene, the child doesn't blame the mother but instead accepts that he forgot to put the uniform where the mom expects to find it. The child recognizes he didn't do his share of the job, so is more willing to accept the natural consequences even though he is angry and says the consequences are "stupid."

This acceptance does not happen naturally. And it doesn't happen easily. This is not about easy or difficult children. We must teach our kids HOW to carry out their responsibilities–first, by having *expectations* that they carry out age-appropriate family tasks; secondly, by *guiding them* as they practice their tasks; and thirdly, by allowing them to *live with the consequences* when they don't carry through. Afterall, our real job is to prepare them for life on their own.

When children are taught how to engage in activities that provide a balance between their interests and needs and those of others, they learn to give, to share, to be part of a team–to take on the shared responsibility for being a family member, a good friend, and later a member of a community.

When everything children take part in is for themselves only, they learn that life revolves around them; *my* play date, *my* birthday party, *my* practice, *my* music lesson, *my* schedule. And when significant others–parents and teachers–support this prioritization, children come to see themselves as overly important and entitled. This entitlement can translate to seeing themselves as "better" than those who don't have such privileges.

While individual interests and needs are certainly important– children do need birthday parties, playdates, and other special events just for them–learning the give and take of working, playing, and living with others is also extremely important in order to live a successful, balanced, and happy life. No doubt, you've already been talking with your children about how to be a good friend, how to share, how to be "nice" to others, etc., but talking and explaining is only part of teaching.

Children must experience being a contributing part of a group, and parents can begin that experience by creating activities for children to do within the family. Again, we start when they are littles. We can hold the expectation that each of our children has a home job that benefits everyone in the family: clearing the table, feeding the cat, bringing their clothes to the laundry room, etc.

When my husband and I were raising our three daughters, each regularly carried out age-appropriate jobs, and it seems that one in particular, shocked my best friend into taking action in her own family. My friend recounted, with humor, her memory of dropping in for after-dinner coffee and witnessing the following scene.

> *My friend and I were sitting at the un-cleared dinner table sipping our coffee and talking. She describes watching my five-year-old putting on her little apron, carefully taking the dishes from the table and putting them on the kitchen counter. Then my friend elaborates on her amazement as she watched my daughter climb up on her step stool and proceed to rinse and stack the dishes. My friend goes on to say she marched home that night and told her five-year-old to put on her apron and get to work.*

Of course, my friend exaggerates, but the message is clear–even incredibly young children can be contributing family members. By engaging children in small tasks as soon as they're capable of doing them, we're teaching our children how to take part in being responsible for contributing to family needs and comfort. In this way, our children are beginning to learn that life is about everyone and that we are each responsible for our share. They learn that their parents, especially their mother, is not the only one responsible for the chores that must be done to keep a household running smoothly.

Did this task always go smoothly with my five-year-old following through on the nights the job was her turn? Absolutely not! Some nights I'd hear whining.

"I'm too tired. It's too hard for me."

"Oh, Honey, I'm sorry you're so tired. It's really hard to do a job when you're tired. I'll help you get ready for bed and tuck you in."

If she agreed, I knew she was indeed too tired. More often, she would change her mind and declare she *guessed* she could do it.

Many evenings after dinner when my sweet little five-year-old complained about the job being too hard for her, I wanted to "do the job for her." I often had a tough struggle between my mother emotions that wanted to rescue her and my intellect that knew the job was age-appropriate practice in life skills she would need as she grew older.

For every family member to have time and energy to play–have a friend over, visit others, do something together as a family–everyone has to take a share in the household tasks and we parents are the ones that must set and follow up on that expectation. Through creating age-appropriate activities and holding our children accountable to carry out their responsibilities in the family unit, we're providing them with the experiences necessary to learn how to become a responsible, contributing member of a group.

~ ~ ~ ~

The importance for shared household tasks addresses the first two steps in teaching children how to become responsible:

> I. Teach them How to Do It Themselves
> Through practicing the activities parents plan, children learn *how* to take care of themselves.
>
> II. Teach Them How to Take Part in Life Outside Themselves:
> Through these types of activities, children learn how to contribute to the shared responsibility of being a member of a group; a family, a school community, a sports team, a club, or any other group. They are also learning that they are not the *center* of the universe, but instead, an important *part* of the universe.

Returning to the parent/teacher comparison, we remember that each new learning skill is most effective when there's a specific lesson plan to refer to, and when that plan begins with a clearly stated learning goal:

Each of us in the family will do one or more tasks that help the entire family.

The goal is reinforced when we give information:

Because each of us is a part of our family, each of us has some responsibility toward helping everyone else.

Sometimes parents require a specific task such as getting up on time, and other times parents can create a list of age-appropriate tasks that will be learning activities for each child. This allows children to choose from that list because it's human nature to prefer choices over orders, and most kids respond more positively when given a choice. This is a good time to point out one or two things Mom and Dad already do each day. You've been modeling these responsibilities, but they probably have not noticed.

- Now is the time to demonstrate how to do the task
- Now is the time to give encouragement as the children practice doing the task

Just as some students don't follow the classroom teacher's directions, so too, children don't always follow our directions correctly, and they most certainly don't follow consistently. Encouragement is telling and describing what the children have done successfully. And, above all, it's always avoiding those negative comments that are so ready to slide right off the tongue and create a battle.

As we continue to guide and give encouragement and support, we still need to repeat and (may need) to add more information. As you continue with the guiding, supporting, encouraging, and a day or two goes by, you will notice something discouraging; your child "forgets" parts of the task and sometimes even "forgets" the task completely.

Don't–*I repeat*–don't do the job for your child.

Now the hard part of this whole process begins; keeping our cool, making the time to carry through on each step for as long as it takes, and–at all costs–avoiding those seven subject-changing and responsibility-blocking parent comebacks mentioned in the Step I chapter.

Our goal is to stay focused on the subject at hand which is to *always* teach our kids how to become responsible. Now, here are some of the particularly tempting comebacks in this type of situation, ones that are sure to be so familiar that they have probably *already* slipped right out of your mouth. No matter; just avoid them from this point on.

> "Feed the dog, NOW." **(ORDERING)**
> "If you don't get your job done, no cellphone for two days."
> **(WARNING)**
> "Is forgetfulness your middle name?" **(SARCASM)**
> "You're just being lazy." **(CRITICIZING/JUDGING)**
> "This is your job. We all have jobs in this house, and if one of us doesn't do his or her job we all suffer.... **(LECTURING)**
> "Come on Mike, feed the dog. He's hungry. Come on, let's get to it. **(NAGGING)**
> "What you should do in order to get the job done is get up earlier." **(GIVING ADVICE)**
> "Why didn't you feed the dog?" **(WHY QUESTION)**
> *And here is a new one to add to the list*:
> "How would you like it if we didn't feed *you*?"
> **(MORALIZING)**

Notice how each one not only changes the subject, but also has the strong potential for creating a power struggle. And–yes–I've added two more since chapter one.

Now, as you take in the information discussed so far, you may be feeling overwhelmed just thinking about all the time this process is going to take. And it does–especially in the beginning. Here's the great news though–as our children learn the process for taking responsibility, they become better and better at it. And the time we must invest in working the process reduces. Our listening time should not be reduced, however. We must continue to learn who our evolving adults are as they grow—a most important process which will help us to communicate effectively with them as they become more independent and responsible.

The hardest part for us is to consistently learn to avoid the power struggle dynamic, stay focused on the goal, and employ the communication-building statements instead of the communication-killers. The second hardest part is doing it and feeling comfortable with doing it.

The following scene is a possible scenario demonstrating how a family might carry out this processing beginning with the task planning, through the initial "honeymoon," and on into the "disenchantment" phase.

Getting the Kids on Board

Task Planning and Giving Information Phase (Steps 1, 2, and 3 of the plans include communicating the boundaries and the choices available for the children within those boundaries)

> "Your Mom and I believe it's important for each of us to take on a share of the work in our family. We've made a list of things you kids would be able to do now that you're ___ years old. You get to choose one of them—one that will be the special job you do for the family."
>
> *If your children are older than five, expect lots of groans.*

At this time, the parameters are laid out: the expectations, the ground rules, boundaries, limits, etc. Sometimes it works for parents to establish them, and other times it works well for parents and children to collaborate to make the rules. The one rule that is uniformly firm is that each person agrees to making certain his or her job is done faithfully, and if there is a time someone must miss his job–say like a dentist appointment, a practice, or sickness–that person makes arrangements with another family member to temporarily swap a task. Be forewarned, however. The process will not go smoothly.

Seven-year-old Jonah decides he'll choose Feeding the Dog, and you employ Step 4 and demonstrate your expectations as you give more information by explaining what that job entails:

> "...every morning before school and every night before dinner be certain to give only one scoop of dog food and refill the water bowl. Wipe up any spilled food or water with a paper towel and throw the paper into the trash."
>
> *Notice the detail of the expectations.*

The Honeymoon Phase – The Feel-Good Part

Then, for the first several days, you model and guide by at first doing the task *with* Jonah, then gradually allow him to take on each part of the task as you observe and give encouragement.

> "I can see that Spot loves to see you filling his water bowl. See how his whole behind wags when he sees you every morning? Your attention helps him to feel so good."
>
> *(Notice that you describe exactly what is happening rather than sharing a judgment like, "good boy.")*

Disenchantment Phase – The Really Hard Part

Now, it's a few days later, 6:30 am. Everyone's rushing around getting ready for jobs and school. Spot is whining and barking. Jonah slumps into the kitchen, and Spot increases in volume. Jonah ignores him.

You are going to be very tempted to give reminders, but that's really called Nagging:

"Time to feed the dog," *and five minutes later,*

"I told you, it's time to feed the dog."

You are going to be sorely tempted to moralize. "How would you like it if we didn't give *you* breakfast?"

You might even be dying to issue threats of consequences or perhaps a sarcastic quip wants to slip out. Hold back, and instead stick to giving *information* and *encouragement*. Remember, this is the hardest and most important job you'll ever do. Take a deep breath!

Usually this is enough to get the young one back on track, but sometimes the issue can become hardcore. What do you do then?

> "I hear Spot telling you he's starving," you say, stating the facts without judgements.
>
> Jonah replies, "Yeah," and just sits there.
>
> "Are you okay, Bud?" (*This is encouragement and support because you're recognizing that he may not feel well*.)
>
> "I guess so," he responds, and you give him "wait time." (*You stand, looking at Jonah and wait for, maybe, 30 seconds.*)
>
> "What? What'd I do?" he asks defensively.
>
> "I'm just feeling bad because I can see how hungry Spot is," you say.
>
> (*Offer information only and offer it in the I statement format.*)

"Rebellion Stage" – The Extremely Hard Part

Begin again at the beginning. But first, a suggestion based on my own experience: Take a deep breath and remind yourself that parenting is the hardest *and* the most important job we'll ever do. I even say to myself, "My job is not to *force* my child to do something. My job is to *teach* my child how to become responsible."

With these thoughts, after your last bit of information is shared, let whatever happens happen, and if Jonah still doesn't take his responsibility to feed the dog, then you might calmly, but firmly, try something like this:

> "I can see you don't want to do this job right now, so what do you say we talk about it tonight after dinner and try to work out a plan that benefits everyone?
>
> "In the meantime, Jonah," you continue, "I'm very concerned about how hungry our dog is. Even though I know it's hard for you this morning (*tone of your voice must show you truly do understand*), I expect that you'll still feed him until we can have our talk."
>
> *(You're putting your child's feelings into words, inviting him to talk further at a convenient time, and restating the expectations.)*

Follow up Talk:

That evening start by giving information and be careful not to lecture. Put feelings into words when appropriate and ask the What question, instead.

> "I'm very concerned about what happened this morning with Spot. Feeding him is your responsibility to the whole family. What do you see might help us to solve this problem?"
>
> *(The question keeps the responsibility for the task on Jonah.)*
>
> Jonah's jaw is set. "I hate that job. It's too hard. I don't want to do it anymore."

Remember that a most important part now is to observe and listen (Step 5) so you'll learn how to be a more effective parent for this particular child. This means hearing more than just words. What have you just heard from your son? Hear his feelings. Put the feelings into words.

> "Sounds like you're discouraged about this job," you say with real empathy in both tone and facial expression.
> "Yeah," he says, "he's always hungry and all he does is whine and bark every morning and every night."

Now, of course, you know this isn't the case, but your objective is to learn what your child's frustration tolerance is. By listening openly, watching his body language, and not engaging his anger, this is what you are learning. You probably don't *want* him to feel this way, but he's telling you how he feels. That's important. So, what do you do next?

You support and encourage him by continuing to put his feelings into words.

> "It's hard to hear that noise every morning, isn't it?"

You are not agreeing with him; you're acknowledging what he's feeling. Continue with your positive observations. Describing the positive is encouragement.

> "I notice that as soon as you feed him, he stops and for the rest of the time he wants to play with you, or he wants to sleep at your feet. Funny how just feeding him makes him love you even more."

Wait time is in order again. Usually, the response to this encouragement is that the child feels better and says he guesses he can do the job. If he still balks, ask him again what ideas he has to solve the problem of how the dog will be fed. You can even offer some of your own ideas–not advice–just a couple of ideas to help keep the responsibility for choosing the solutions on the child.

The boundary in this situation is that the dog must be fed regularly, so a solution to the problem must be found. For children to learn how to become responsible, they have to experience coming up with ideas of their own rather than being given advice from others. When parents merely add a couple of their ideas along with the child's ideas, and then together discuss each idea, the child is freed to make his or her own decision and learn from the outcomes.

Remember Step 6? Repeat the process as often as it takes for your child to get it. And when children don't carry through with their responsibility for that task, they must live with the natural or logical consequences–Step 3–that were put in place when the task was created.

~ ~ ~ ~

I can hear many of you right now saying, "Are you kidding me? My parents just said, 'Feed the dog or you're grounded.' So, I fed the dog, or sometimes I didn't, and then I was grounded. The dog was healthy, and today I'm a responsible person!"

And you probably are a responsible person; however, we know something now we may not have known when you were growing up. Children are more likely to take on responsibility consistently and positively when parents take the position of Lead Parent by guiding them, rather than that of Boss Parent who demands it of them. One of the main reasons this is the case, is that Lead Parenting models how people engage in responsible problem-solving and how people work together to solve problems. Boss Parenting does not encourage or even allow for a child to learn how to problem-solve.

If the *purpose* of the activity called "Feeding the Dog" is to give the children practice in becoming responsible for the task and others they've agreed to do, and if the *goal* is contributing to the family's needs, then we must model responsible actions ourselves.

We have given information; we've listened and observed; we must model a *responsible reaction* even when we're feeling frustration and anger. We model a caring, yet firm, resolve to discuss and work on the problem at an appropriate time, hopefully that very day.

This does not mean that Jonah "gets away" with not carrying out his commitment, but rather that he learns how to go about solving an issue which is a most important life skill.

Once an alternative way to feeding the dog is chosen, it's tried for a short while and then revisited to see how it's working. The Boss way is faster and often feels much easier in the moment, but it doesn't show children *how* to take responsibility. Because the Boss Parent Model is the most familiar parent model for most of us, learning how to become a Lead Parent may seem unnatural in the beginning. For this reason, it's of great concern to parents, so please note that Section VI of this handbook is all about this topic: "Expect Obedience or Teach Them How to Work Through a Power Struggle."

Just as we expect our children to carry out age-appropriate responsibilities that contribute to the family unit, we also expect them to carry out their responsibilities in other groups. As our kids grow, they become members of sports' teams, clubs, etc., and effective parents continue teaching their kids how to become responsible by showing them how to be contributing members of these groups.

The school community is probably the largest other group. We hold the expectation that our kids do their schoolwork and are respectful to their teachers. If our kids join a school club, we have the expectation that they attend the meetings regularly and that they do a share of the club's work. If they join the chorus, they take part in practices and performances, same for sports' teams.

We expect them to be kind and considerate to others; their group of friends, strangers in the school community, as well as to all school staff–janitors, lunch people, office people, teachers, and administrators. Sadly, I have experienced many adolescents who actually believe the janitor's job is to pick up after the students. A valid question arises: What have their parents been modeling?

Part of being a member in any group is learning how to address issues that arise. There are always issues wherever people get together. Instead of solving these issues for our kids, we do the same thing we did when we addressed the issue of feeding the dog.

We ask the people involved to meet with us and our child to discuss the issue. And the best part of this process is that at this point in our children's lives, we're right there to guide and support them–all the while modeling how to address issues and work respectfully with others.

A particularly threatening area for us as parents occurs when we believe our kids are being treated unfairly. Naturally, we want to jump in and "rescue" them from unreasonable teachers or from a school or neighborhood bully. How we handle these situations models one of two ways to work with others: either we model the way to be a productive team/group member OR we model the way to manipulate others to get what we want, often at the expense of others. If we model the second way, we are teaching our kids to see themselves as more important than others.

The following are typical issues kids often face. As you read each,

> **9th Grader**: "That teacher is so unfair!"
> **Parent**: "What happened?"
> **9th Grader**: "I thought my paper was due the 9th and now she says the 5th. I'll never get it done on time. She's always changing due dates on assignments. There's no way I'm getting a good grade in that course."

pretend this is your child talking to you. Take note of your immediate response to each.

What was your response? Did you immediately want to take care of this for your child? Did you want to call the teacher right then and find out why s/he was "so unfair?" How about this next situation between your child and a group of other students?

> **5th grader**: (*comes home after school terribly upset*) "One of the kids at school said I'm fat, and he was making fun of me. Then, in the lunchroom, he got a bunch of kids to walk by my table and whisper 'fatty'. I'm not going back to school anymore!"

Aren't you just itching to call the school and that kid's parents and let them know the kid is a bully? Here's a more productive plan: first, we calm the raging Mother or Father Bear instincts.

We do that by reminding ourselves of our main job; teaching our kids how to become responsible, and that means learning how to become responsible for addressing their issues. Throughout their elementary and high school years and experiences, parents have something going for us that will not be available after high school. We're *present* to model how to address issues in a constructive way.

A huge bonus of these issues our kids face is that, when we deal with them responsibly, they offer strong "teaching moments." To use these teaching opportunities effectively, everyone involved can meet– the teacher, school counselor, or the coach, along with the other child's parents and any other children involved. At the meeting, someone describes the problem without blaming anyone; they just provide information. Then everyone can discuss together by adding information and asking questions. The goal is to model how to address issues and then to help the kids learn one or two skills for how to handle such a situation more successfully in the future.

The Rest of The Story

Here's what happened when the people involved met to address the two previous issues. In the first incident, the parent and child learned that the assignment had been posted online and that the rough draft was due the 5th and the final paper the 9th. Once the missing information was identified, the teacher and the parent were able to work with the student on ways to make sure s/he had all the needed information for future similar situations. In the second incident, the parent contacted the school, and the school made an arrangement for a school counselor and all parents and the children to meet and address the issue.

During that discussion everyone learned that a week earlier, the child who was being taunted had been bragging that she was smarter than "those dumb boys." As a result of this meeting, the school counselor decided to have a series of sessions in which the students learned and practiced social skills regarding how to talk to other kids when they were angry.

Do such meetings always solve the issue? Not at all, but everyone learns "the rest of the story," and usually a skill or two to deal with future issues. *In addition, the adults can model a process for how to take personal responsibility and how to interact with others in what is often a difficult situation.* In situations where the issue remains unresolved, the adults must model how to live with disappointment, anger, and frustration responsibly.

The importance of fully collaborative meetings really came to me during a devastating "parents only" meeting with me, their son's teacher. The parents refused to have their son, a high school junior, attend the meeting. They arrived expressing great anger. They wanted their son's grade changed from "C" to at least a "B" to keep his average at what they saw as high enough for his college transcript.

They opened the meeting with strong blaming statements.

"We are disappointed with your teaching. You have been totally inflexible and unfair to our son."

They continued to describe my unreasonable attitude when their son had missed an appointment with me. After all, they said, he was busy with sports and that, "typical of kids," he just "forgot." They told me I was doubly unfair because I refused to let him make up missed work. They asked no questions and were not open to any discussion.

What these parents could have learned here was that the boy had not come for help despite our having made several appointments, and while the boy had asked to make up work, he had done so after the grades closed, and he had learned his grade was a "C."

Most critically, what they *might* have learned was that their son felt he had to lie and manipulate situations in order to make himself acceptable to his parents. What the boy might have learned if we'd have had a *student*-parent-teacher meeting is that although he messed up, which is something all human beings do, there are more effective ways he could have dealt with the situation. And it would have given him tools to use in future situations.

This meeting was not a discussion to address the issue. It was an attack to get what they wanted. Their goal was to manipulate me into changing the grade. When that didn't happen, they resorted to verbal bullying by threatening to have me fired.

What were these parents teaching their son about becoming responsible for his own actions? What were they teaching him about being a contributing member of a group and to living with rules that held all students to the same expectations and consequences? What were they teaching him about how to live his life?

In my professional opinion, the fallout from this episode was devastating to everyone–to the parents because they were teaching their son that lying and manipulation are the only tools to success and devastating to me because I cared deeply for that student.

But the real harm done was to that beautiful human being–their son. He was learning that getting what he wanted is more important than honesty and that consequences only applied to those in the class who could not manipulate their way out of them.

Let's look at a constructive way this meeting might have progressed. First let's assume the boy had indeed told his parents the same lies in an attempt to cover up for his own irresponsible decisions.

Then let's see what might happen when the boy comes with his parents and when the parents, although probably still angry, avoid blaming and present the issue as they see it. Again, notice the teacher employing the What question in this scenario. Since the young man is a junior in high school, he opens the meeting. He is old enough to carry out that responsibility.

> **Boy**: "Well, we're here because I have a 'C' in your course, and I need a 'B' for my college transcript."
>
> **Father**: "We're all very upset about this grade. He tells us you refused to let him make up work he missed when he had swim meets at other schools".
>
> **Teacher**: "Sam, I have three dates here in my calendar that you and I planned to meet so you could make up missed work, and you didn't come in. What happened? Would you say more about that?" (*No blaming, just state the factual information.*)
>
> **Sam**: "I don't know. I couldn't make those times. I had a practice or something, and I know I forgot one of them. Sorry about that."
>
> **Teacher:** "Tell us some more, Sam. What happened when you learned your grade was a 'C'?"
>
> **Sam**: "I asked if I could make up my work and you wouldn't let me."
>
> **Teacher**: "What's your understanding of the reason for my decision?"
>
> **Sam**: "You said the grades had closed."
>
> **Mother**: "So now you're telling us Mrs. H. had made arrangements for you to make up work, and you didn't keep those appointments?" (*No blaming – just stating what she heard*)
>
> **Sam**: "I guess, but I was really busy."
>
> **Father**: "I want to be sure I understand this. You didn't ask to make up work until *after* the semester ended and you found out you had a "C"? You haven't been completely honest with us here." (*Again, just stating facts*).
>
> **Sam**: *Looks down at the table saying nothing.*

This meeting could go differently. The boy could deny he had lied and continue to insist the teacher was unfair. It doesn't matter as long as the parents are modeling how to handle a difficult issue without blaming anyone, *including their son*. Once everyone has explained and asked questions, the next step is to talk about how to handle such a situation in the future.

> **Parent or Teacher**: "Sam, at this point the grade has to stand, so the next step is for us to figure out a few steps you can take so this doesn't happen to you again. Does that sound like it might be helpful to you?"
> **Sam:** "I guess."
> **Teacher or Parent**: "Do you have any ideas? (*No lecturing or solving the problem for him*)
> **Sam**: "I don't know."
> **Teacher or Parent**: "Could you leave a note when you can't make a meeting?" (*This is just a suggestion here; he doesn't have to take it*).
> **Sam:** "If I have time, I can. Sometimes the team has to leave in such a hurry, I don't have time." (*Pause.*) "Maybe I could text Mrs. H. after we're on the bus."

The meeting continues until two or three ideas have been agreed upon and written down.

No one is blaming anyone for anything. Sam lied to protect himself. That issue can be dealt with later. What he needs for this *present* issue is to learn life skills that will protect him in the future. Our job as parents–and teachers–is modeling how to interact and treat others respectfully even when we're angry. For kids to learn the value of *all* people, we have to model the process. Remember, modeling is the strongest teaching skill known.

When do we begin this type of expectation? The answer is, right from preschool. Whenever we meet with teachers or parents of other kids, include the children. In the early years, *we* arrange the meeting, and do most of the talking (modeling), and gradually, as our children get into grade school, we turn more and more of the meeting over to them. If the child is developmentally ready, by high school, s/he is initiating and leading the whole process. By this point, if we've done our job, our child may not even need us to be at the meeting.

~ ~ ~ ~

In addition to modeling and teaching our children how to take age-appropriate responsible action for their share of family and school involvement, we need to model and teach responsible action in other areas such as in our neighborhood, our community, and with the environment.

How do we teach this broader responsibility to children? As with all teaching, we follow the plan: we give information; we model; we create the learning activities that engage our children in the learning; and we guide and support, never giving up.

Parents can plan all kinds of age-appropriate activities for learning how to carry out these types of responsibilities and then ask children to choose ones they can do. Of equal importance with *my* game, *my* birthday party, *my* activities, *my* plans are the ways we can contribute to something outside ourselves.

A few examples might include arranging for our children to make cards for a hospitalized neighbor, to call a friend who stayed home from school with a cold, to write thank you notes, to volunteer at the library or our place of worship, etc.

The most effective plans we can make are, of course, for ourselves to become active in our own volunteer work. Remember parents are always modeling and, when age-appropriate, it's powerful to invite our kids to join us. Tweeners and Teeners can volunteer at a veterinary clinic, a hospital, their school; the list is almost endless. What do we do for the environment? Whether it's recycling, buying a car with greater gas mileage, buying low energy light bulbs–whatever it is, we can include children in the discussions of such actions and engage them in the activities.

The goal for our children to live as responsible and empathetic group members is met through many and varied learning activities. Our own creativity and love of fun are available to help us to create new and varied ways of involving our children. When we take the time to teach our children how to become responsible for things outside themselves as well as how to become responsible for their own decisions and actions, we're teaching them the essential life skills of building and maintaining healthy relationships with others–and with themselves.

We're teaching our children to be a caring and responsible part of the world rather than the center of it.

TOOLS # 2

Review & Continuation of Communication & Responsibility-Blockers

<u>Review</u>:
1. Ordering
2. Warning
3. Using Sarcasm
4. Criticizing/Judging
5. Lecturing
6. Reminding/Nagging
7. Giving Advice/Solving the Problem for the Child
8. Moralizing

Comments on the "What" Question vs the "Why" Question

"Why didn't you get your room cleaned as I asked you to do?" (Do we *really* want to know what the excuses are?)
Instead, ask the What question
"What are you going to do to get your room cleaned today?" (We *do* want to see a plan in action. There may even have been a good reason why it hasn't yet been cleaned, but our expectation remains the same; the room will be cleaned today.)

See the difference? Not "why" didn't you do it, but rather, "what" is your plan for doing it *now*?

Check out some of the scenario examples on the following pages.

The Missing Information

As I worked with my own children during three-way meetings, I learned that in almost every situation there was "missing information." Just realizing that this would no doubt be the case helped me to stay calm enough to model and guide effectively. The following are a few examples from my experiences as a mother, a teacher, and a grandmother.

I Hate My Teacher

2nd Grader: I hate Mrs. Thomas.

Parent: What happened? (The "what" Question)

2nd Grader: She won't let Tamika and me sit together at the same table.

Parent: Sounds like you're feeling sad and angry. (recognizing her feelings)

2nd Grader: I'm really mad at Mrs. Thomas! She moved us for no reason!

Parent: I wonder why she did that. (Wait) How about you and I ask Mrs. Thomas? (only a suggestion)

2nd grader: What if she gets mad at me for asking?

Parent: I think we can explain to her that we just want to understand. (Give Wait time)

2nd Grader: (Pause) Well, (Pause) I guess so ... (another pause) if you're there, too.

Parent: We can talk to her together.

What I learned when the three of us met is that Mrs. Thomas moves students around so that they experience working with different students. We were able to teach Cheryl to ask the teacher whenever she didn't understand why something was being changed.

~ ~ ~ ~

The Teacher Doesn't Like Me

7th Grader: "The Drama teacher took my part away from me! And I've spent so much time learning it."

Parent: "Oh Honey, you must feel so disappointed." (*Recognize her feelings*)

7th Grader: "Mr. Fitts doesn't like me. He gave the part to Lilli."

Parent: "I'm so sorry." (*Pause for Wait Time*)

7th Grader: "It's not fair."

Parent: "Have you talked with Mr. Fitts to let him know how much you want the part?"

7th Grader: "It wouldn't do any good."

Parent: "Would it help if we talked with him together?"

7th Grader: "No, he'd just say he had reminded me."

(*Now, my mother-ears heard something that didn't fit with the opening of this conversation*).

Parent: (*Remaining calm*) "Reminded you of what?"

7th Grader: "Oh nothing, just forget the whole thing."

Parent: (*Sitting quietly to give wait time*)

7th Grader: "Well, I guess he reminded me I had to get my lines learned."

Parent: "Oh." (*More wait time*)

7th Grader: "I guess he thought I wouldn't have them learned by Friday night when the play goes on."

Parent: (*Still sitting quietly, paying attention, and waiting*)

7th grader: "Maybe I should have learned them earlier. Lilli had them learned before I did."

Parent: "Are you thinking you would do it differently next time?" (*Putting into words what the child just said*).

7th Grader: (*Pause*) "Yeah, probably I didn't learn them fast enough."

Parent: "I can see how hard losing the part is for you, Hon. I hear something else too—something good. I think you're saying that next time, you'd do things differently. You'd do whatever you're responsible for earlier." (*No blame–just putting what you heard into words so your child can hear it*)

In this example, we didn't even need a meeting. I found the missing information merely by listening to my seventh-grade daughter. Listening is a very critical skill for a parent.

> **Larry Called Me a Terrible Name**
> **4th grader**: "Larry called me a dirty Jew and said he was going to beat me up!"

What Sam's parents learned by meeting with Larry's parents along with the two boys: First, Larry's parents were very upset that Sam's parents would see them as prejudiced. In the discussion, they learned that Larry had heard this language from an older boy and not from his parents.

Then Larry explained that he was mad because Sam had stopped playing with him after school. During the meeting, the parents were able to teach both boys some productive ways to handle this type of situation.

> **Terribly Inconsiderate 10th Grade English Teacher**
> "That teacher is so inconsiderate. She didn't even listen when I tried to explain I couldn't get my work done because we had an away game. Now I have a zero and can't make it up."

What Sarento's parents learned when they had the three-way meeting was that the teacher had given the assignment several days earlier because she knew many of the students had upcoming sports responsibilities. In the meeting they were able to brainstorm together a few alternative and responsible ways Sarento could handle any similar situations in the future.

When Your Child Lies to You:

You have just learned that the party your sixteen-year-old daughter, Samantha, went to last night–that same party your daughter repeatedly assured you would be chaperoned by both her friend's parents–not only had no parents present, but the party included alcohol.

You are way beyond mad, and you cannot even voice the disappointment you feel in your daughter.

Dad & Mom: "We've just learned that Raol's parents weren't at the party last night and that there was drinking going on."

Samantha: "But I thought his parents would be there."

Dad & Mom: "And when you found out they weren't there and that there was alcohol, what did you do?"

Samantha: "I didn't know they weren't there."

Note that Samantha is sticking with the issue she believes she can win.

Dad & Mom: "What did you do, Samantha?"

Note how the What Question keeps everyone on the topic.

Samantha: "I told you, I didn't know they weren't there. I thought maybe they were up in their room or something."

Dad & Mom: "What is our rule about parties?"

Samantha: (*raising her voice*) "But I didn't know they weren't there."

Notice the parents don't change the subject by mentioning her yelling at them.

Mom & Dad: "A large part of being a responsible person involves checking to make sure events you take part in are within our family rules. You haven't commented on the fact that alcohol was served. Frankly, we're feeling very disappointed in the choices you made regarding this party."

Notice also that the parents gave information–no lecture–described their daughter's behavior and stated their feelings rather than using any of the responsibility blocking statements.

Samantha: "But, I didn't have anything to drink."

Dad & Mom: "You know the rules, Samantha, and you know that enjoying privileges is directly related to taking responsibility for your actions. You made a choice to stay at the party and not ask where the chaperones were. You made a choice to stay at the party when alcohol was being served. This choice put you in a lot of potential trouble for many reasons, but definitely because it's against the law. We're going to take your cell and your computer for one week and during that time we want you show us that you are able to make responsible choices."

Samantha may react by yelling, "Now I'll just fail school because you won't let me have my computer," or she may run to her bedroom and slam the door, screaming, "I hate you." She may just say "ok," but don't count on it.

More reasons to use the What Question:

It works wonders toward helping kids recognize and take ownership for their behavior.

It keeps us from using the responsibility-blocking comments that stop constructive conversation.

It prevents the subject from changing. It keeps us on track.

It might go something like this: Your son has agreed that his job is mowing the lawn, and today is the day for that job. You come home and find the grass is just as tall as it was this morning.

And where is your son? Joyfully playing video games, totally oblivious to the growing grass. You may be about to lose it, so you take a deep breath and confront him with a What question. (And yes, it is reasonable to have a bit of an edge in your voice.)

The Lawn Dispute

Parent: "What are you doing?"
Son: "I'm winning," he replies without looking up from the screen.
Parent: "What are you supposed to be doing this afternoon?"
Son: "What do you mean?" he asks, eyes still glued to the game.
Parent: "I want you to tell me what you're *supposed* to be doing."
Son: "Damn, now you made me lose that one!" He's looking at you now!
Parent: "What did we agree you would do today?"
Son: "Awe, come on. I was just taking a break."
Parent: "What did you agree to do right after school?"
Son: "I said I'd mow the lawn, and I will," he says, getting to his feet and starting out the door.

Parent: "Thank you. I know it's hard to come home and go right to work, but that was our agreement," you say, acknowledging his feelings.

Yes, this could escalate into something more–rudeness, storming off to his room, etc. but that is another subject, and it is best dealt with separately. Meanwhile, you have held your son and yourself to the subject, you've avoided responsibility-blocking and potentially hurtful statements, and your son has defined what he is supposed to be doing, confirming that he is aware of his agreement. And yes, this is a scene that will be repeated because learning to become responsible is a process. It takes time.

Catch yourself every time you start to use the *Why* Question...

"Why are you just sitting there with your phone when I asked you to empty the dishwasher?"
"Why aren't you doing your homework?"
"Why did you go to Noah's after I said not to?"

...and replace it with the *What* Question:

"What are you doing?"
"What did you do?"
"What are you supposed to be doing?"
"What was our agreement?"
"What time were you supposed to be home?"

When we ask the Why Question, we're *encouraging* our kids to provide an excuse.

When we ask the What Question, we provide a path for them to take responsibility for their choices.

STEP 3

THIRD STEP TO CREATING *IRRESPONSIBLE* KIDS

Overlook *Their Unacceptable Behavior*

If we've told them once, we've told them a thousand times to hang up their things, be home on time, do their homework, let the dog out when they get home from school.... No matter what it is, they just forget about it, and we end up doing it.

Our kids each have a job to do when they get home from school, but most nights we come home, and nothing's been done. So, before dinner gets started, the dishwasher has to be emptied, a load of wash needs to be put in, or whatever else they didn't do.

And homework–we won't even go there. Whenever we ask if they've done it, they say yes, and then we find out they may have done *some* of it. We used to check their homework, but now they are older, they refuse to let us, so we've just turned the responsibility over to them.

We can see that all our nagging, lecturing, threatening, ordering and all other things earlier mentioned as "not to do" don't work either. And even punishing them doesn't work. We have grounded them, taken away their electronics, made them miss an important event, and, yeah, sure, after they've been punished, they do their work for a while, but then they start "forgetting" again.

And frankly, even when we sit down with them and follow the "lesson plan," it ends up not working. We give information, create the activity, demonstrate, and then guide, encourage, observe and listen– they still don't continue to do what they're supposed to do!

The older they get, the harder it seems to be.

Nothing works with today's kids. We are so ready to give up.

THIRD STEP TO CREATING *RESPONSIBLE* KIDS

Teach Them How to Deal *with Uncomfortable Consequences*

I feel your frustration. Parenting is the hardest job we'll ever do. Here's the thing though, if giving up worked, we wouldn't have Step #6 in the lesson plan, "Repeating everything as often as it takes and never giving up." Parenting is the most important job we'll ever have.

What do talking on the phone, going somewhere in the car, having company, going shopping, leaving the children with a sitter, all have in common? These are times when, for sure, our kids are much more likely to engage in "not-so-positive" kid behavior. They'll bicker and fight, constantly interrupt our phone conversation, bug us in the store to buy everything, convince the sitter they can watch that forbidden TV program, etc.

Back to the lesson plan, Step 1–what is the learning goal? Yes, even during our preoccupation with our phone call or family needs, we can teach a lesson in how to become responsible.

The learning goal might be, "Our children will learn how to show respect for another person who is busy."

You know the drill now, so what information do you want to give? Think back to the detailed expectations needed when explaining how to do a particular job such as feeding the dog. Clear expectations are especially important, right? With this in mind, we know that children need to know the meaning of the words in the learning goal. There's a particularly strong teaching strategy we can use here.

We ask our kids to join us in brainstorming what a particular word, such as *respect,* "looks like" and "sounds like." The following is an example of what the end results might be.

Looks Like	Sounds Like
Looking at the person speaking to you	Quiet, because we stop talking when Mom or Dad asks us to stop
Not making a face or rolling our eyes	Saying, "Okay, Mom/Dad."
Following the rules when Mom and Dad aren't home	Getting a good behavior report from the babysitter

Making the list is usually fun, and it can be as short or as detailed as you and your children decide. Then it can go on the refrigerator for future review, too. Just like those goals-in-progress.

What's next? We move onto step 3 and explain the consequences that will result after the first few "practice" sessions.

And, because we know children will most certainly make mistakes, we make sure we're there to guide and encourage them as they live with those consequences, especially the uncomfortable ones.

Just as they must practice learning to be responsible for tasks and behaviors, they must also experience the appropriate consequences in order to fully understand the results of their choices.

In section "Step 1" we looked at the definitions of two kinds of consequences:

Natural Consequence: Something that would "naturally" occur as a result from a person's behavior. For example, getting a zero on a test if the student missed it because of an unexcused lateness or absence.

Logical Consequence: Something that would be a "logical" result from a person's behavior. Examples of logical consequences might be having to go to bed earlier in order to be able to get up on time or losing a privilege until responsible behavior is shown. Losing a privilege is logical because privileges come with the demonstration of responsible behavior.

The main difference between Natural and Logical consequences is that *logical* consequences are those *we* determine in order to preempt a *natural* consequence. Although natural consequences are strongly effective, *sometimes* they are not age or situation appropriate.

Please, Daddy, I Won't Do It Again

Say, when you go to the market for groceries, you usually stop for ice cream on the way home. Your child knows that if s/he doesn't carry out the learning goal–to listen to you and behave well–there will be no treat.

> **Dad**: "Okay, Son, we're going to get some groceries for dinner."
> **4-year-old son**: "Oh boy! Do we get to have an ice cream cone on the way home?"
> **Dad**: "Well, what's the learning goal for going to the grocery store?"
> **Son**: "I know it, I know it! To show respect to you in the store and if you say no, I can't keep asking."
> **Dad**: "Right! Let's go, Big Guy."

Now, in the store, he asks for a toy and you tell him, "not today," and he continues to whine. Perhaps you remind him of the learning goal by asking him about it:

"Jeremy, do you remember what the goal is for shopping behavior?"

He ignores you and continues to beg for the toy. Take a breath. You've got this. You vehemently avoid those judgmental statements. You don't issue the classic warning, "If you don't stop, we won't get ice cream."

You avoid ordering him to stop right this minute. You don't lecture or explain that you only have enough money for groceries today. You continue shopping, pay for your groceries, and go home without ice cream.

This consequence could be considered both a logical and a natural consequence. If your child has not shown respectful behavior, the natural outcome is that you are tired out from his whining, and you just want to go home. However, the consequence that you created and the one the child understands is that if whining continues, there will be no stop for that ice cream cone. What's most important is that a) you don't lose your composure, b) you don't give in, and c) the activity and the consequence is age-appropriate, and the lesson goal will eventually be accomplished.

Natural and logical consequences work most effectively because kids understand them. They may not like them, but they see that their behavior and the real-life outcome of that behavior are connected. There are *many* natural and logical consequences. For example, if the children are fighting in the car, the natural consequence is that you will need to get home quickly because it's dangerous to drive with noisy distraction. Monash University in Australia released a study in 2013[10] that stated, "children are 12 times more distracting to a driver than talking on a mobile phone while at the wheel."

Because everything is clearly stated ahead of time, the learning goal and the consequences, there is no need for discussion at the time. It would be reasonable to give one reminder, using what is known as an "I-Message."

For example, "I am really having a hard time concentrating on my driving when you guys are fighting. I expect you to stop, and we'll solve any issues later." It's just fine if your tone expresses firmness and even frustration.

I know you're probably thinking, "Get Real. I have to get groceries and I have to take my kids with me, and most of the time, it's an exercise in frustration. And I don't have time for managing their learning goals right now!"

Believe me, I understand, but let's try to stay focused on our ongoing objective; to teach our children how (a process) to become (over time) responsible individuals.

Let's look at "business as usual." We threaten, "If you guys don't stop fighting, no TV tonight." They're quiet for a minute or two, and then it starts again.

We threaten again, "Do you want me to stop the car right here and give you a spanking?" And of course, they know we aren't going to do that, so the threat isn't a concern.

Next, we order *and* threaten, "Stop that fighting right this minute, or you're going to be in big trouble." They ignore us.

We criticize, "You guys are acting like animals."

And so on through the whole list of judgmental comments. As things escalate, we usually end up saying something really foolish, like, "Okay, I have had it! You are grounded for a month!"

We are in survival; we are not parenting. In the moment, we're frustrated and angry. All too often we end up over-reacting and saying things we don't really mean. Our kids know we don't mean them, too. So, the learning objective has become, "Children will learn to ignore what parents say."

Another, and equally ineffective way we avoid dealing with consequences is to *overlook* our children's behavior. We give information that tells them our expectations and even the consequences if they don't carry out the learning goal. But, when they ignore the goal, we act as if we never held the expectation in the first place. This approach may be more peaceful in the short term, but it teaches our kids to ignore others' needs.

One of my very good friends, Meg, invited three of us over for lunch. She explained to her four children that she would be making their lunch at noon, and she expected them home from their friends' houses on time because her friends were coming at one o'clock. She further explained that if the children were late, she would not be able to get their lunches and they would have to make their own. Meg had certainly given clear information and clear natural consequences.

At noon, three children presented themselves, but Scott, age twelve, didn't show. At one-thirty, he arrived home and asked his mother for lunch, whereupon she left our luncheon table, telling us she'd be right back after she made a sandwich for her tardy son.

WHOA. STOP. REWIND THAT SCENE.

What is the worst thing that could happen if she stayed at the table with her friends and told him to fix himself a sandwich? A messy kitchen? A less than completely nutritious lunch? Maybe a whiney son who helplessly keeps calling from the kitchen asking where everything is?

If we think in terms of the learning goal in this lesson, we see that the *intended* goal was "If Scott isn't home, he will take the responsibility for making his own lunch so his mother can enjoy time with friends."

That objective quickly changed, becoming "If Scott isn't home, he really doesn't have any responsibility because he can count on his mother to give up her own needs and make his lunch."

The most important ingredient for helping her son learn to take on his responsibility of respecting someone else's needs is the *consequence* that follows. If the consequence is that Mom will do it, then he learns to ignore another's needs. If, on the other hand, the consequence is uncomfortable, he will learn that taking expected responsibility is more favorable than not doing so.

Of course, having to make his own lunch can't be described as actually uncomfortable, just inconvenient perhaps. This lesson may not have ended yet. What if, after the friends leave, Mom discovers a real mess in the kitchen? What is a real-life natural consequence here? Obviously, it's Scott's having to clean the kitchen, but what if Scott has already left to spend the night with a friend? A perfect opportunity for Scott's lesson to continue.

Meg can give him a choice to come home and clean up the kitchen now or to clean up the kitchen after dinner for the next couple of nights, assuming this is not his regular family job anyway. The point is that because he didn't take responsibility for cleaning up in the first place, leaving Mom to do it, he will make it up by going above and beyond as a thank you to his mother for doing his job for him.

Why not a punishment? Let's go back to our overall learning goal–to teach our children how to become responsible. When we issue a punishment, we change the learning to "teaching our children to do as they're told."

When we institute natural and logical consequences, we're teaching our children how to become responsible, and we are modeling skills needed for maintaining successful relationships. When Meg expects her son to make restitution for inconveniencing her, she's providing the learning experience for him to practice one of the most important skills for maintaining a successful relationship: demonstrating thoughtfulness and respect for others.

Let's further examine the two types of consequences mentioned previously; natural and logical. If our goal is to teach our children *how* to become responsible, we want to allow for *natural* consequences as a first outcome. When waiting for natural consequences takes more time than is developmentally appropriate, we may decide to incorporate *logical* consequences.

Thinking back to Scott's not returning for lunch on time, the natural consequence is that he prepares his own or goes without. The logical consequence of his leaving a messy kitchen is that he makes restitution to the person who cleaned it up.

When do you use natural versus logical consequences? Let's say your second grader hasn't completed his math homework this week, and it's now Wednesday. The *natural* consequence is that he may well get a low grade on Friday's test. Do you allow him to wait for further *natural* consequences? Probably not at this age.

A *logical* consequence is the appropriate step at this point. An example could be that he does his math homework every day *with you* until the next one or two test grades show he knows the work. Age, developmental readiness, and the type of situation are key in deciding which type of consequence is appropriate.

Let's examine this type of situation with an older child. It'll be more of a challenge if your child is a middle or secondary student. She may not even see a problem–may tell you, "no big deal, just had a bad week." For this reason, the best way to begin is to listen to how she feels about the situation. If she seems to be blowing it off, here's a possible scenario (Note two communication skills to use–you have seen them before; "I-Message" and "Paraphrasing.")

> **I Can Handle It**
> **Daughter**: "There's no big deal, Dad. I'll take care of it."
> **Dad**: "You believe it isn't an issue right now, so you don't need any help."
> (A*void those judgmental statements and keep the responsibility on your daughter by* **paraphrasing** *what she just said into your own words to check that you understand correctly.*)
> **Daughter**: "Yeah, I'm fine with it. I can take care of it. You'll see when I take next week's test."
> **Dad**: "You know, Honey, I'm not feeling good about this; in fact, I'm worried. I'd like us to come up with some things you'll do *this* coming week to help you do well on that test."
> (*The* **"I-Message"** *lets you state your thoughts and feelings and what you want.*)

Your daughter may "hear" your concern and put it into words, but don't count on it. You have been modeling this for years, but she is an adolescent which is generally synonymous with self-absorbed. It's much more likely she'll give you attitude.

> "I *told* you, I'll take care of it," followed by an eye roll.
> "What's your plan, Honey?" (Use a What question to help keep things on track.)
> "You always want a *plan*. Don't worry about it. I don't need a *plan*."
> (Deep breath.) "I need to know you have a plan. Let's brainstorm some ideas, and you can choose the one you like best. (Stay with the I-Message format to keep communication clear and open.)

Let's assume she refuses to work with you. Which kind of consequence do you choose? If you go with the *natural* consequence, you may tell her you are willing to give it one more week and see the test results. If you decide that *logical* consequences are more appropriate in this case, you might give her a limited choice:

> "Because I see this problem as so very important, I'm going to give you a choice. You can sit down right after dinner every night next week and do your math homework here where I can help you when you need help, or you can do your homework any time during the day and then let me check it for you right after dinner."
> (*I Statements, no blame, no criticism, and offering reasonable choices provide the best opportunities for success in this tough conversation.*)

If your adolescent refuses to choose, you can make the choice for her. Then comes the hard part in this lesson: the "carry through." With your own busy schedule as well as the needs of the rest of your family–not to mention your own–following through may be extremely difficult. But it is critical to the success of this process.

Let's suppose she flat out refuses to comply with the choice you made for her. Now you choose either the natural or the logical consequences depending on your child. If you and your child have a history of getting into ugly power struggles, choose the natural consequences. I wish I'd had this information when my oldest was a teen.

Now, as much as you hate to let go, *do it anyway*. Tell her you're sorry she's making a choice to go it alone, that you believe it is not a beneficial choice, but that you wish her the best in her work. Be genuine, not sarcastic. Then, remembering the last step in a teacher's lesson plan, never give up. Assure her if she decides she wants help, you will be there for her.

Why, you may be thinking, wouldn't I just walk away and let her fall flat on her face? The answer is especially important–you're modeling responsible behavior in an interpersonal relationship. The fact is no person can *make* another do something, and when we attempt to do so, we're modeling how to engage in a power struggle. When this occurs, both people are left with bad feelings, and over time, the relationship suffers. It's the quintessential example of a lose-lost scenario.

"But she'll probably just keep on failing her tests! I can't let her do that," the parent cries.

Yes, with a very headstrong child, you *can let her do that*, and you *must let her do that* if she insists on making the wrong choices. She's *practicing* how to become responsible and right now you are there to guide and encourage her. If she fails and you refrain from inserting any of those judgmental statements, especially the "I told you so" type, she will be more open to realizing on her own that her choices were poor ones.

Saving face frees her so that she's much more likely to turn to you as she lives with the uncomfortable consequences and then to allow you to guide her, help her pick up the pieces, examine her choices, move on, and make a plan to become successful the next time.

When we try to force the issue with demands and/or punishment we might win some of the battles, but we deprive our children of the opportunities to learn the necessary steps in the process of learning how to become responsible.

Steps In Learning How to Become Responsible

> 1. Recognizing a problem or denying the problem
> 2. Trying a solution or continuing to ignore the situation
> 3. Having to deal with the outcomes (consequences) or celebrating the outcomes
> 4. Starting over and, if needed, being able to accept help

The more natural the consequences, the stronger the recognition of the connection to the chosen behavior.

If you and your child have little to no power struggle history, s/he may respond positively to logical consequences, and if this is the case, you might calmly respond to her refusal to choose one of the choices you offered with something like, "I'm sorry you don't like the choices I've offered. You are free to find an alternative, but until your mom and I know you have brought up your grade, we expect you to come home from school and study here each day."

You're probably used to thinking of discipline in terms of punishment, and if that's the case, it's more difficult to realize the power of natural and logical consequences as a form of discipline as opposed to punishment.

If our goal is truly to teach our children how to become responsible, then we must discipline by holding them accountable to consequences that match their behavior. Let's consider consequences as opposed to punishment as we look at another scenario, this one of a young child from my own family.

My third-grade granddaughter was eating her breakfast, and her mother gave her a bowl with a little brown sugar in it, telling her she could put half the sugar on her cereal. She didn't follow her mom's instructions and ate almost all the sugar. When her mother confronted her, she vehemently insisted she had eaten only half.

Now her mother's job is to carry out a consequence. She can issue a *punishment* such as no TV this evening. She can issue a *natural consequence* such as allow Alana to experience a negative reaction to the sugar.

She can issue a *logical consequence* such as no afternoon snack when Alana comes home from school.

To analyze this case, let's ask ourselves what the learning goal was here. The answer is that Alana has been in the process of learning to make healthy, responsible choices with food. Now we can consider what type of consequence is going to further that learning process:

- **If** her mom issues a punishment of no TV this evening, Alana experiences no connection between her choice to eat all that sugar and the punishment. Furthermore, her learning goal has become "Alana will do as she's told"
- **If** her mom issues a natural consequence in this situation, the possible results are too damaging and take too long
- **If** her mom issues a logical consequence, Alana will experience the connection between her actions, the learning goal remains the same, and, in this situation, the logical consequences preempt the probable negative effects of the alternative choices

Now her mom can choose a logical consequence that matches Alana's goal of learning to make healthy food choices; she may tell her there'll be no after school snack because she has already eaten her sweets. With the logical consequence, she experiences no harm, and she experiences the connection between her choice and the consequence.

This scenario assumes that Alana and her mother have been in the process of meeting this learning objective–that information has been provided, discussions have been held, and this incident is an example of allowing Alana to practice taking responsibility for healthy eating by following her mother's direction. When she makes the unhealthy decision, she must live with the related follow-up; a consequence that continues her learning because it's related to making healthy eating choices.

She protested loudly and with a stamp of her foot shouted, "That isn't fair!"

So next, Mom guides and encourages her daughter through the unwanted consequence. Mom's response might be something like, "I understand that you really want an afternoon snack" (putting her feelings into words), "and next time you have a choice to make, I'd like you to think about how that choice might affect the rest of your day." (giving information with the I-Message).

Who carries through with guiding Alana after school when both parents are at their jobs? Communication to the after-school caregiver is essential. It is the carry-through even though it's another thing to have to remember to do.

There are endless opportunities to help our children learn how to deal with uncomfortable consequences: when they don't do their homework, when they neglect to put their dirty clothes in the laundry, when their rooms are messier than is acceptable, when they "forget" to be home by the agreed upon curfew, when they throw a party while parents are away for the weekend, when they aren't at their friend's sleep-over like they had said, or when they do just what we told them not to do.

One of my own most monumental moments in teaching my children how to become responsible happened while my middle daughter was a high school junior. It was a most painful experience for us but we both learned a great deal from going through it.

What happens when your daughter who has just earned her driver's license "borrows" your new car even though you told her "No"? She not only deliberately defies you in taking the car, but in attempting to back out of the driveway, she  puts the gear into Drive and slams into the garage door.

Mad? There are no words to describe how mad I was. My daughter deliberately ignored my needs, the garage door was ruined, and my brand-new car was severely damaged.

I stood there in the driveway, taking many deep breaths, and, in my most controlled state, created an I-Message.

"I'm so mad at you right now I can't even talk about this. Until we can talk further, I want you to think about how you're going to take care of *all* the damages."

And I walked away.

> **The Aftermath**
> **Me**: "I'm hurt, I'm disappointed, I'm furious, and I'm worried."
> **Kristin**: "I'm so sorry, Mom."
> **Me**: "I know you're sorry, and I appreciate your telling me, but we have three huge problems here. The first and most important one is trust between you and me. I trusted you to honor my needs about my things, and now I don't feel that trust. The second problem is the cost for a new garage door, and the third problem is the cost of the car repair.
> "The last two can be fixed fairly quickly and we'll discuss how. I'm most concerned about the trust issue. That part will take time to repair."
> (*Again, using I-messages and information with no blaming helped me not to react emotionally which would have been disastrous.*)

Then, I stopped talking. I just looked at her and waited. She had many more "I'm sorries," and we cried, and I waited for her to offer some ideas of how to begin to solve our problems. In her adolescent wisdom, she assured me not to worry about the car and door repair "because that's why we have insurance."

I can tell you that on that day, and the many that followed, she learned strong lessons about how life works–that insurance has a deductible, that making a claim will probably raise the premium, that it would take her *a year* to pay this obligation from her part time job, and most of all, she began to learn that breaking the trust held between people in a relationship takes a long time to repair.

After the first few weeks of Kristin's giving me part of her meager salary, I started to feel miserable. Hadn't she learned her lesson? Shouldn't I just tell her to forget the rest of the cost? My husband and I discussed this endlessly. We struggled between what we knew in our heads and what we felt in our hearts. We forced ourselves to carry through until she had paid all the deductibles. It took a full year.

The harsh consequences are, of course, the hardest to get through for everyone. All these consequences were indeed natural ones and became positive experiences in the long run. Because she made restitution, Kristin was able to repair some of her damaged feelings of self-worth. Because I held her to the consequences, I experienced a deep pride in her determination to complete the restitution. I saw a strength in her that I had not seen before, and I think she realized it too. As for repairing the trust in our relationship, I know she took that most seriously. Never again did she do anything to jeopardize that trust.

Along with holding our kids to the consequences of their poor choices, it is vitally important that we also help them recognize and celebrate the consequences of their positive choices: when they have faced harsh consequences and worked through them, when they've carried through on that school project, when they've earned that desired grade, when they've fed the dog consistently for a week, cleaned their rooms, been on time for school…. Even when the responsibility is one, we, as adults, might expect our children to know, we need to verbally recognize their positive choices and do so on a regular basis.

Just as we describe what our child has accomplished so far during a particular task, so too, we recognize our child's completion of a task by describing the positives we observed, "I am proud of the way you handled that difficult situation. You kept your cool and worked to get a solution. That took a lot of self-discipline." This type of encouragement goes a long way in reinforcing our children's positive choices.

In life, every choice we make has a consequence, even a little decision to sleep just fifteen minutes more on a given day. As adults, we are so used to making choices, we often don't even think about them, but children *are learning about choices*. The very fact that they do have choices and that each choice has a consequence is a monumental lesson for children in the process of learning how to become responsible people.

Let's Do a Little Review

Before moving on to the second half of this handbook, let's think about the first three ways we create *IRRESPONSIBLE* kids:

I. Do Everything for Them
II. Expect Nothing from Them
III. Overlook Their Unacceptable Behavior

Now let's think about the three ways to create *RESPONSIBLE* kids:

I. Teach Them How to Do It Themselves
II. Teach Them How to Take Part in Life Outside Themselves
III. Teach Them How to Deal with Consequences

Why is the second set of alternatives so hard for us? Yes, our culture does promote the first set, and these first ones are so much easier in the moment. BUT there's a deeper reason. Doing everything for our kids can, and usually does, make us *feel and look* like nicer and better parents.

When our children don't play well in the game, or they get a poor grade, or they struggle with friendships, or they get into trouble at school, or they deliberately refuse to carry out our expectations, we experience a nagging little voice that tells us *we've* somehow failed.

Immediately we want to make everything right, so we do things *for* our kids instead of *teaching* them how to do those things for themselves, or we blame our kids or others for the problem and don't hold our kids responsible for their actions. Our "help" (and our anger) becomes more about *us* than about our children.

We genuinely want our children to succeed but we also want to succeed at being good parents and to be seen by others as good parents.

Letting our children struggle, even to the point of allowing them to fail at something while we guide and encourage them as they go through the consequences is truly more difficult for us as parents than for our children.

TOOLS #3

Review of the I-MESSAGE

Simple I-Message

The simple I-Message is a statement with no judgment, blame, advice, or any of the other blockers and begins with I:

"I'm sorry you have to have this consequence."

"I can see you're really upset about this."

"I (we) see this situation differently."

"My observation is that your clothes are on the floor and your bed isn't made."

Extended I-Message

There are three parts:

1. Describe what is happening	"When you are fighting in the car, _____."
2. Say what you're feeling	"I feel _____ (distracted, scared, worried)."
3. State what you want/expect	"I expect you to stop right now."

"When you haven't emptied the dishwasher, and I have to do it myself before I can even start dinner, I feel overwhelmed. I expect you to do it now and to remember to do it in the future."

In this type of situation, we begin a statement with the word, *you*, and we end up *Ordering, Blaming, Criticizing or Judging, Warning/Threatening,* or *Lecturing.* Whenever we put others on the defensive, we shut down *all* opportunity for anything positive to happen.

Parents have often asked me, "What's the point in saying how I feel?"

Well, sometimes an I-Message can be an invitation to solve a problem when used with a What question:

"When you tell me that you're going to Nisha's house after school, and instead you go to the mall, I feel betrayed and lose my trust that you'll tell me the truth. What can we do to change this?"

The goal is to prevent us from using any of those responsibility-blocking statements which will not help the conversation or the situation.

My mentor, Marian, told me of a time she was first learning to use I-Messages with her teenaged daughter, Lynda. One particular night, Lynda was supposed to have put on the chicken to cook so it would be ready when Marian came home from work. That isn't what happened.

That evening, returning home from work, tired and late, Marian didn't smell anything cooking, and before she could stop herself, blurted out, "Where's the chicken you were supposed to start cooking?"

Her daughter immediately became defensive and yelled, "Well, I have this big test tomorrow and I forgot. Okay? I'm not perfect!"

Then Marian remembered how she wanted the conversation to go and shared her feelings with Lynda. "It's just that I'm so disappointed."

Marian relayed the rest of the story to me, and I will never forget it. She said that Lynda stopped what she was doing–and the strangest thing–she offered to take care of dinner and even apologized. She seemed to realize immediately that her mom wasn't blaming or criticizing her, but rather, she really was tired and "disappointed."

Of course, it does not always go this well, but we stand a much greater chance of promoting successful results when we avoid the responsibility-blocking statements. Try it out!

Showing empathy by putting other's feelings into words (Introduced in Step I)

> "I can see how angry you are about this."

In addition to showing you understand, using this responsibility-building skill helps kids recognize their own feelings–something that isn't easy for them.

Showing interest and attention by putting other's words into your own words

This skill is often called *paraphrasing* what the other has said. It's a great way to check your *understanding* of what was said. Caution here: Avoid beginning the paraphrase with the word *you*.

- "So, what you're saying is _____ (and you paraphrase)"
- "Are you saying you would prefer _____?"
- "If I'm understanding what you mean, you would like to _____"
- "Let me see if I understand what you want in this situation." (Paraphrase your understanding.)

Many times, we may not like what we're hearing from our child/adolescent, but we model this skill anyway and work to take our child seriously. Remember, they are learning from us as we use these skills. Modeling is the most powerful of teaching methods.

- "If I'm understanding you correctly, you're saying your job is going to school, and you shouldn't be expected to do anything around the house because you're too overworked now." (This is a perfectly logical conclusion to many teens and will lead into a discussion of shared responsibilities.)
- You believe it's your mom's and my responsibility to buy you a car because all your friends' parents are buying them cars.

Essential Process for Using These Three Skills

As you interact with your child/adolescent, especially in potential power struggle situations, create a mental image of your child with two speakers, one on each side of her/him. One of these speakers transmits ideas and plans (words) and the other broadcasts emotions (feelings). At any given moment, one of these speakers is *louder* than the other.

Your job is to discern *which* one is louder at any given moment and respond accordingly. And the hard part is that they can change *very* quickly. Let's continue with an example from above.

Your fourteen-year-old daughter has just asked to go to a party this upcoming weekend. You hear ideas and respond by paraphrasing what your child said. This process of recognizing the louder "speaker" and then responding to it appropriately is a very difficult skill to master. It may take years, but we parents can speed up our learning by applying it in discussions with each other as well as with our children.

The Would-Be Party

Mom: "So what you're saying is this party is a big deal and all your friends are going."
Daughter: "Yeah, everyone is going."
Mom: "Sounds like fun, Honey. We do have a few questions about the party."
Where upon your child switches speakers and responds with
Daughter: "What questions? Don't you trust me?"
You hear emotions in this one, so you respond,
Mom: "You're feeling that you're old enough to handle this responsibility, and you want us to trust you on that."
Daughter: "Yes. Everyone else's parents are okay with it."

Mom: "Well, if we can clear up any questions we have, then we won't worry, and the party will be fine." (*I-Message*)
Daughter: "Okay. What? I can tell you right now, Nisha's parents will be home and there's no drinking."
You identify ideas and maybe a tinge of emotion, but ideas are louder. You continue,
Mom: "That's great. And we'd like to know that if any drinking starts, you'll call us to come and get you."
Daughter: "Oh, Mom, that's so juvenile. I wouldn't do any drinking so what does it matter?"
Mom: "What matters is that drinking is against the law for minors, and if anyone got hurt, you could be implicated."
Daughter: "OMG! That's not going to happen. You worry about *everything*."
Mom: "We know you feel this is overprotective." (*Responding to the emotion speaker*.) "The thing is, these are the parameters we're comfortable with, and if you go to the party, we expect you will respect our needs." (*Stating your expectations*)

The Technique of Providing Choices

The key to offering choices is that each one must be a *real* choice, not a "choice" between doing what they're told or being penalized. Just the same, please do not expect your child to always be delighted with her choices. For example:

"We aren't negotiating whether you'll put your book bag away. We all put our things away. Would you rather put it away when you come into the house from school, or wait until you've had a snack?"

Logical consequences are not always met with acceptance.

Making Amends[11] or Restitution

When kids have to make restitution rather than serve a punishment, they see the direct connection between their actions and the consequences. In section III, Scott would need to make amends if he left the kitchen a mess. My daughter had to make restitution by paying the deductibles for the damage to the garage and my car.

Describing Positive Behavior and Naming the Trait *We Observed*[12]

- I see you put your book bag on the peg every day this week. I would call that *being responsible*. I'm proud of you.
- Wow, today I see you put five toys on the shelf. That's *being helpful*. Thank you.
- I noticed you shared your candy bar with your sister. I think that shows a lot of *generosity*. I'm proud of you.
- I noticed that for the past few days you've fed the dog all on your own and then cleaned up any messes he made. I'd call that *dedication*. Way to go!

By doing this, we are telling our kids just what they did that was positive rather than using a generic statement like "good boy" or "good girl" which might leave them guessing about exactly what they did or said that was "good." Catch them doing good things and encourage them by letting them know you noticed.

Defining Words in a Chart

Looks like ____	Sounds like ____

STEP 4

FOURTH STEP TO CREATING *IRRESPONSIBLE* KIDS

Fill Every Moment for Them

It's Friday and you are leaving work early to get your youngest to the pediatrician in time for her booster shots. Hopefully, she will not get a reaction because she has an important game tomorrow.

Instantly, you realize you haven't made the arrangements for your three children's Saturday sports schedule. Glancing at your pocket calendar, you see that Jerome's game is at eight am at the town fields, Javica's is at ten am at her school, and Tatianna has an away game at three pm.

While driving to pick up your youngest from school, you make a quick call to your spouse to make arrangements for sharing the driving and to make sure one of you can attend each game. You pull into the parking lot at Tatianna's school, shut off the car, and go inside to pick her up. She's waiting for you, bubbling over with excitement about the new girl in her class.

"Can I invite her to my birthday party?" she asks.

Then you remember that *sometime* on Saturday, the ice cream cake must be picked up, and this reminds you that Jerome's trumpet has to be picked up on Monday–before five, and you already have plans to leave work early on Monday to take Javica to her math tutor. You do not even dare to think beyond Monday because you know that every afternoon and some evenings are filled with scheduled lessons, practices, play dates ... and the reality hits you that this familiar routine will continue to cycle through every week and weekend *for the next ten to fifteen years!*

You inhale deeply hoping to de-stress. You want your kids to have every opportunity. You'd probably even feel guilty if you did not make sure they participated in everything available for them. Your thinking is along the lines of many of the following parent thoughts:

- If my kids don't begin playing a sport right when they start school, they will never get picked for a team; we have to make sure they are enrolled by preschool.
- Sports are so healthy mentally and physically, we want to make sure our children are in a sport every season–soccer in the fall, swimming and basketball in the winter, lacrosse in the spring, and swimming again in the summer.
- In our area, a foreign language isn't taught until 7th grade, and we want our kids to start earlier because it's easier for them when they are young. We've found a wonderful tutor who teaches languages through games and play, and Gabby loves her language play dates.
- Juan is so musical, and he chose the instrument he wants to learn so he can play in the school orchestra. There are two concerts a year, and it will be incredibly good for him to perform in public.
- Mavis really isn't being challenged by her classes–almost no homework and she's still making honor grades. She should be in IB classes, or at least, in AP classes.
- And friends? We make certain our children are very involved with other kids. We plan play dates for them, swimming parties, sleep-overs, camping weekends. In the summer, we find wonderful craft camps, sports camps, music camps, and so they don't forget what they learned in school over the summer, we enroll them in tutoring classes.

Juggling all our children's activities is chaotic, stressful, and very time consuming and expensive, but in the long run we know it's worth it.

Or is it?

FOURTH STEP TO CREATING *RESPONSIBLE* KIDS

Teach them How to Make Healthy Choices

Yes, all these activities are important to a healthy childhood and all these events can create healthy bonds between parents and children. Here's the catch though–in grown up life, people must choose certain things and forgo others. Because we have obligations, we can't do everything we might want to do, and we must plan how we can incorporate a healthy balance between "have to" and "want to."

But parents might be thinking, children should be exposed to everything, so they know what they want to choose when they grow up.

Having a wide variety of activities is a wonderful thing, but far more important is the responsible life skill of making choices and planning when and how to carry them out in a way that creates balance within *all* areas of life.

For children to learn *how* to carry out this process, they must practice it. We parents must teach them by guiding them through the process as well as modeling it through our *own* choices. Again, we return to the lesson plan, and yes, we will have a lot of lesson plans going on at the same time.

Create and discuss Step 1, the learning goal. Some parents keep a list of the learning objectives their children are working on and post it on the refrigerator.

"This quarter, Jevante will learn how to narrow his school activities to _____ (two, three–you choose based on his developmental stage) and he will learn how to balance those choices with other areas in his life."

Reviewing the teaching process:

1. Write out the learning goal: state the objective
2. Plan the activity: fosters practice of the goal
3. Establish consequences: discuss natural and logical
4. Demonstrate or model the goal ourselves. Give examples
5. Guide, encourage, observe, and listen
6. Repeat (over and over and over!)

Teaching the process of making healthy choices may be the hardest of all the steps in teaching children how to become responsible because we may not have learned it ourselves. We can give information forever, but if we're not modeling it in our own lives, the learning we intend will not take place.

Are we ourselves working too many hours and not balancing work with family? Yes, I know we may well believe we are working all those hours for our family, but, again, modeling is the strongest teacher known.

Are we playing all weekend and not balancing our play with family obligations? Are we modeling quiet time, alone time, hobby time, family time, conversation time? Are we talking with our children about the choices *we're* making in our lives? Are we expressing our disappointments in not being able to do all the things we want to do, and modeling how we alternate our choices so that we can eventually do *almost* everything we want to do–just not all at the same time?

To prepare children for making responsible activity choices, parents can lay the foundation throughout preschool years by giving lots and lots of information and creating activities with their child in a way that models balance through making choices. With this experience, by first and second grade, most children are ready to make some of those decisions themselves, but with lots of continued guidance and modeling and with continued limited choices. This process takes great parental courage, but also yields great payoffs.

All My Friends' Parents Are Letting Them Do It

Give information and create the learning objective.

> **Mom**: "Millie, your dad and I've been looking at a list of all the activities going on this year with your school, and it looks like you're going to have a lot of possible choices to narrow down to the two you want to do this fall (*the learning objective*). Let's look at the booklet together and talk about what interests you the most (*the lesson's activity*)."

As you look through together, you give any additional information, including other age and developmentally-appropriate parameters you and your spouse have established.

Continuing, you and your daughter read the choices and discuss the inviting pictures of children playing soccer, swimming, performing in the talent show, playing in the band, etc. And, of course, Millie wants to do it all.

You give support and guidance through a response that recognizes her feelings and sidesteps all those *Roadblocks to Communication and Responsibility*. You stick with the boundaries while continuing to put her feelings into words.

> **Mom**: "It's very hard to make only two choices when there are so many exciting things to choose."
> **Millie**: "But, Mom, I could do more..." (*and she spins a plan she believes in, but you know is impossible even for a magician.*)

> **Mom**: "Everything here sounds so exciting, and I know you really, really want to do most of them (*putting her feelings into words*). For this fall though, we have to narrow it down to two. In the spring, you get to choose two of the others."
> **Millie**: "No, that's not fair! (*her little voice becomes a loud and demanding big voice*). There's no reason, and all my friends' parents let them choose as many as they want."

You bite your tongue because you are modeling how to stay with the process–no changing the subject by mentioning her tone of voice or other parents for that matter.

> **Mom**: I can see how difficult this choice is, and I'm going to let you have some time to look at the list on your own, and when you're ready to decide, just let us know. *And as you calmly exit the conversation, you may hear her say something like,*
> **Millie**: "You never let me do anything. Fine! I won't do anything!" as she, with great dramatic flair, storms out of the room.

What happens if Millie does refuse to do anything as she threatened? The natural consequence is that she'll be extremely disappointed as she watches her friends participating and she's doing nothing.

But her disappointment won't be nearly as deep as your own because you so desperately want her to have these experiences, to learn the skills, and to make the friends she would make by participating in the activities. What do you do now?

You continue to guide and encourage as she copes with the consequences of her decision. When she mopes or cries, you show empathy by putting her feelings into words, but avoid those communication and responsibility-blockers, especially that moralizing one which you may be so tempted to slip in.

"This is what happens when you put off decisions."

Then, remembering that the *effective teacher*–and you *are* one–never gives up, you begin again. If she refuses to choose, this particular practice session will have to wait until the next time activities begin, at the school quarter or half, but there are *many* opportunities for engaging in choices that create balance.

When children get older, the task becomes even more difficult, and if you've waited to begin this lesson until the children are middle school or older… well, we won't even go there. Just be prepared for–at the least–lots of eye rolling, and at the worst, volcanic rumblings and eruptions. It's just a fact that adolescents don't like change, and they especially don't like their *parents* to change. By the time they are heading into their teens, they have learned how to "deal" with the way you have always handled things, and now you're taking them into unknown territory.

With older children, parents can continue to offer choices, increasing them as appropriate for each child. If your older child is rather accommodating, you'll probably eventually have success in offering limited choices, but it's a different story if your tween or teen is a rather "usual" adolescent, meaning self-absorbed and determined to be independent.

In these situations, the process can become oh-so-time-consuming because your task is to lead your child to see for himself that he cannot do it all. When this is successful, the learning is much greater. Let's look at a possible scenario with a fifteen-year-old. It may be helpful to review lesson plan steps 5 and 6 in order to keep your cool during this learning activity.

- **#5 Guide, Encourage, Observe, and Listen**
  Stick with the Responsibility-building language.
- **#6 Repeat, never giving up**

The following scenario picks up from where your (now) teenage daughter has informed you that she can choose *everything* and still be successful. Keep in mind the *reason* you are about to carry on the following discussion.

Your goal is to lead your child through a process during which she comes to the realization that her initial desires are not reasonable and that she does indeed have to make choices. Understand that this is your goal, but it may not happen. That's okay. Interact with that goal anyway because you are modeling a process and it will help to keep everyone calmer.

> **Mom**: "I'll tell you what, Millie. You show us on a calendar how you can play soccer, take both piano and dance lessons along with practicing each day, do your homework, carry out your family jobs, have time for family and friends, and include a healthy amount of sleeping and unscheduled time. Oh, and remember we all have to work around one another's schedules."

Even though this is an impossible task, by the next day your daughter has it all worked out, so you resume your conversation. She wrote it on the calendar that she now confidently and proudly presents to you.

There it is, all neatly written out, and she has included everything. Dance and piano on Mondays, practicing both every day for an hour at 5 am before school, swimming on Tuesdays, soccer practice the other afternoons, her home job right after dinner, homework every night at 8:00 pm – maybe 9:00 or 10:00 if there's an important TV show (most teens see no problem with saving time by sleeping less–that is until it's time to get up). Oh yes, and she can get together with friends at school and on weekends.

Now, you immediately see all the issues here, *but* remembering our parent objective of teaching our children *how* to become responsible, we take our child's thinking seriously.

Mom: "I can see you worked really hard on this schedule, and you organized everything very clearly. (*Acknowledge her thinking and planning.*) I have some concerns and questions, but I'd like to start by listening to how you see all of this working out each week."

Millie breathlessly starts: "I've figured it all out, Mom. I can do the dance lessons and piano lessons on the same day if you pick me up after school and take me."

(*This sounds very plausible. So, you give information again.*)

Mom: "I don't get out of work until 5:00, so no one can pick you up from school earlier. What time were you thinking would work?"

Millie: "Well, you could take me when you get out of work."

Mom, providing more information: "That would be the same time we're getting dinner, and remember Monday nights are when our family does something together after dinner."

Millie: "Oh yeah, well how about Tuesday night?"

Mom: "That might work. (*Wait time.*) What would you do about the swimming that's on Tuesday night?"

(*Use the What Question to keep the responsibility on her and to avoid the word* but *to sidestep a "gotcha" situation*).

Millie: "Maybe I could do swimming on Saturday morning?"

Mom: "Yes, that's a possibility. (*Wait time.*) What would you do when there's soccer practice on Saturday mornings?"

Your discussion may continue along these lines while you point out, using questions, the other issues with the plan while she confidently pursues her goal.

As time goes on and on, you are truly wondering just why you're doing this. You're drained. You are ready either to give in and move on or give an emphatic NO and let her storm or sulk it out.

Your thinking is going something like this: "Two days and she still doesn't get it? Why am I wasting my time when I have so many other things to do?" You may even be thinking this method gives a child too much control.

Okay, let's examine these thoughts. You *can* avoid the stress of arguing if you just give in. Besides, in the overall scheme of life, the situation isn't that big of a deal. You can save time by just telling her NO and be done with it. She will be upset, but she'll get over it.

Doing either of the above alternatives will change the learning objective. If you give in, then the lesson becomes, "Millie will learn how to manipulate others by cajoling, pleading, wearing them down...."

If you take over and tell her no and that's that, the learning becomes, "Millie will learn to do as she's told." Of course, someday there will be no one to tell her what to do. Or no one to help her discern what is healthy for her and what is not. If she has not learned how to reason through her choices, handle the consequences, and consider the impact on others, she will never be a responsible, healthy, adult.

You can see that neither of these objectives leads to a child's learning *how* to become responsible. For children to learn how to become responsible, they have to practice the steps, just as they would in learning any other skill. I know I drove my parents crazy when I was practicing the piano and hitting all those wrong notes. And it took me a long time to learn each lesson.

Teaching is tough and very, very time consuming. Millie's learning objective for this lesson is that she will learn how to make choices that create a balance within all areas of her life. Reinforced within this learning objective are all the responsible behaviors discussed and shown in the first two chapters, "Teach Them How to Do

It Themselves" and "Teach them How to Take Part in Life Outside Themselves."

You are teaching her a process and you are teaching her to recognize life outside herself by having to respect the needs of others even when those needs infringe on what she wants. This is not an easy lesson even for us adults.

Assuming that the goal is still to teach her how to become a responsible person, continue the conversation with her by giving information, asking questions, putting her feelings into words, paraphrasing to check your understanding, and listening.

Putting her feelings into words may be the strongest skill you can employ because her hopes and dreams are being dashed here. Something as short as "I can see how hard choosing is, especially when there are other people's schedules as well as your own to consider." You may have an idea or a suggestion but be prepared for her refusal to consider them.

Children have a very hard time limiting themselves because they truly believe they can do it *all*. And culturally, this thinking is encouraged:

"Be all that you can be!"

"The sky's the limit."

"Never let anyone tell you that you can't reach your dreams."

This belief makes perfect sense because they have so little experience in decision-making and in meeting their obligations. That's what we're teaching them through this process.

Another positive outcome of this long-drawn-out process is that, later, when they blame us for not letting them do everything that they want, they begin to hear a nagging little voice deep down inside reminding them that *they* made the decision themselves and with full understanding of why they did. The process *encourages* kids to take the responsibility for the decisions they make–it does not *guarantee* that they do. It does make it a whole lot harder for them to blame others.

Coming to an agreement on how many activities actually can reasonably be included is not enough. The next step is to write it down.

Once a schedule has been agreed upon, we have another critical task to teach and that is how to carry out a schedule. Even our older children 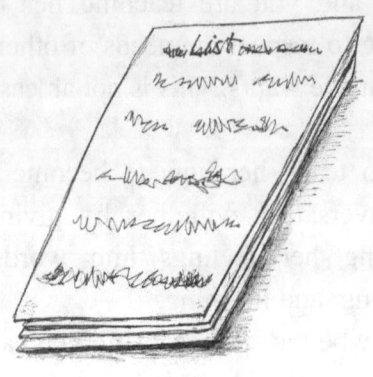 probably don't know how to do this, and for certain they will all get discouraged with it, just as we saw Josh do with having to feed the dog every day.

Everyone can write out their own schedule and be in charge of their own time. And because the children have schedules, we parents can more easily avoid falling into the nagging trap of giving constant reminders.

All we have to do when our kids don't do something they're scheduled to do, is to refer to their schedule. The most successful way is to use only one word: *schedule*.

The fewer words, the less argument, and fewer excuses we're likely to get in response. Besides, when we do get an argument or excuses, we just give the "raised eyebrow" look and say nothing. We've already said all we need to say; "schedule."

This individual schedule includes everything the child is to do each week: lessons, practices, homework time, games, play time, family time, bedtime, home tasks, and unscheduled. Here's an example. See how simply it's done:

Sample Weekly Schedule

After School	Monday	Music lesson, empty dishwasher, homework
	Tuesday	Soccer practice, empty dishwasher, music practice (30 mins), homework

	Wednesday	Music practice (30 mins) empty dishwasher, homework
	Thursday	Soccer practice, empty dishwasher, music practice (30 mins), homework
	Friday	Music practice (30 mins), empty dishwasher
Weekend	Saturday	Games practice, time with friends, homework
	Sunday	Family, friends, homework
	Every day	AM: get up and to school on time & with all needed materials. After dinner: get school stuff ready for the morning Be in bed by _____ (whatever time is agreed upon)

Encourage each child to list as much as is needed for that particular child. You may want to include such things as family time and other personal activities, and remember, a most important activity to include is time to have *no* planned activity.

Some of this unplanned time can even be without TV, without game boxes, without technology of any kind, and even without friends. This is time for kids to complain that they're "bored." Maybe they will read, or draw a picture, or write a poem, or just daydream.

As we teach our kids to balance the myriad activities of life, we often forget to allow them to embrace the magic of doing nothing, often viewed as boredom. To teach this lesson, parents must first allow the space for boredom to enter–a rare occurrence today.

Let's assume you have worked with your seventeen-year-old son in such a way that he has agreed to limit his Xbox 360 games to one hour a day, and today that hour is used up. He wants to save his hour of TV for a special program. He has fed the dog and done his homework. He flops into the kitchen as you're preparing dinner:

> **Son**, sighing: "I'm so bored. I don't have anything you'll let me do."
> *(Be prepared to be blamed because you set a boundary that the schedule had to include unscheduled time.)*
> **Mom**, not taking the bait, gives information: "Boredom is a wonderful thing, Honey. "It's magic."

Now *you're* probably asking the same question he will ask you. "How is boredom magic?"

A big question to ask ourselves is have we learned the magic of boredom? When there is nothing we feel like doing or what we feel like doing is out of reach at that time, we're forced to be creative and that's where the magic is.

A person's response to boredom is often to sit, or even mope, and think about what summer vacation in Maine will be like, about what college next year will be like, about how to get that new guy's attention, daydreaming, composing a song or a short story, painting a picture, reading a book...boredom is magic.

So, with a thoughtful little smile, you offer your son a tidbit of information such as, "I love boredom."

Or you ask a question. "What can you do with boredom?"

Then you leave him wondering and probably thinking you've gone over the edge, but you've planted a seed.

I told you at the start that parenting is the hardest job we'll ever do. But, teaching our kids how to become responsible through the process of learning how to create balance in their lives is so worth the aggravation, the frustration, and the time because we are teaching our whole family how to live a mentally and physically healthy life.

TOOLS # 4

Reminders for the teacher
- Give limited choices.
- Put feelings into words and paraphrase what you hear; *according to whichever speaker is louder.* Switch back and forth as needed.
- Ask questions to lead your child to recognize a situation instead of Telling.
- Allow "wait time" for your child to think about the conversation.
- Encourage as your child lives with the Natural or Logical Consequences of his/her choices.
- Avoid the roadblocks that I call Responsibility-Blockers:
    Ordering
    Warning
    Using Sarcasm
    Criticizing/Judging
    Lecturing
 Reminding/Nagging
    Giving Advice (solving the problem for your child)
    Moralizing

New tools in the Fourth Step to Creating Responsible Kids
- Make individual schedules (Each child makes their own schedule with guidance & support.)

- Avoid using the word *but* because it says, "gottcha" which blocks your child's thinking process and maybe even lead him to think the whole process is a manipulation instead of a powerful process.
- Defining words by "Looks Like" and "Sounds Like"
- Giving One-Word Reminders (*if* you must remind)
  - Schedule
  - Back-pack (for reminding to hang it up)
  - Toys (for picking them up), etc.

STEP 5

FIFTH STEP TO CREATING *IRRESPONSIBLE* KIDS

Solve *all their problems for them*

- "It's the parents' job to protect and take care of their children, right? Our teenage son got a warning stating he has an F in Algebra, and when I asked him what was going on, he said the teacher doesn't like him. I'll have to call her and have a talk."
- "Our 5th grader had a project he'd worked on for three weeks and his teacher gave him a C on it! He's so disappointed, but too shy to talk to the teacher about it. We called her, and now his mom and I are going in to find out what happened."
- "Another problem is how mean kids can be to each other. Someone's always being left out or in a fight. Then we have to call the other parents or contact the school and talk with the principal."
- "After Mark didn't make the team, he was all bummed out and just moped around the house for days. I had to give him the old "Buck up and take it like a man" speech my father gave to me. He stopped talking about it after that, so I guess he stopped feeling sorry for himself."
- "Our kids are constantly fighting with each other. 'She took my sweater and won't give it back;' 'I was watching T.V., and Cory just changed to his show without asking;' 'She's touching

my things;' 'Mavis hit me' (followed by a wail), 'She hit me first.' We've tried everything and nothing works. Sometimes it's so bad, *we* want to run away from home."

FIFTH STEP TO CREATING *RESPONSIBLE* KIDS

Teach *Them How to Deal with Disappointment and Solve Problems*

Dealing with Disappointment

Your fifth-grade son didn't make the "A" soccer team this spring, and you are furious because he has been a really good player ever since he started playing in kindergarten, and he was on the A team last year.

"There's definitely something wrong with this new coach. Assigning my kid to the B team–the man's an idiot!"

Very natural parental feelings. Now that you have recognized your own fury, how are you going to help your son deal with his disappointment and move on?

Simple: you *allow* him to *feel* his disappointment and anger by carefully listening while he tells you about not being chosen. Avoid those communication and feeling blockers and give support and encouragement by putting his feelings into words.

"You really wanted to be on this team, and now you're feeling disappointed and angry because you weren't picked."

At this moment, his feelings are the most powerful aspect of this crisis, so you want your son to know you understand how he feels. A common response when you identify his feelings is that he may cry–very difficult for many fathers. A paramount fear of almost every dad is turning his son into a sissy. Out of this fear, our culture has taught us to tell our boys to "be tough and take it like a man." This approach, believe it or not, is actually counterproductive to teaching children how to become responsible for dealing with life's unpleasantness.

Psychologists and educators now know more about the brain than they did in the past, specifically more about how people process their feelings and what types of responses from others are the most helpful.

These experts inform us that people work through their feelings more successfully when another person responds with empathy instead of with any of the Roadblocks. When someone responds to our feelings with empathy, we feel understood, and that's really what we all want when we're upset—someone who understands how we feel.

Later, after the initial diffusion of the emotions, a person is better able to think, to process information, and to plan next steps. At this later time, we can then offer information or suggestions. If we try to give information to our child while he's buried in feelings, he won't be able to process our information, and we'll probably be accosted with an angry outburst like, "You don't know how I feel."

Once your son knows that you understand his feelings—after all, this *is* the number one worst event in the history of his life (and you may feel the same way)—you and he can have a conversation. You've been reading about how to put feelings into words and to paraphrase ideas. Here's a way to think about how to switch back and forth between responding to feelings and to words as needed.

As the two of you talk, remember to listen to *both* of his speakers—the one expressing his feelings and the other expressing his ideas. Then, respond to whichever is stronger at that given moment.

Whenever you hear the feelings-speaker stronger than the ideas-speaker, put the emotions into words because this helps to defuse his feelings which in turn helps him to think. When the idea-speaker is louder, that's the time to respond by checking your understanding of what he is saying. In other words, you paraphrase what you think he is saying.

Also, please be savvy to the knowledge that this conversation will probably be continued over several days, weeks, or even the entire season, every time feelings may surface again. Your job continues in the same manner; alternating your responses between identifying his feelings when the feelings-speaker is stronger and putting his ideas into words when that speaker is stronger.

To help him be responsible for his next decisions, there are two actions parents can take to ensure they are guiding him. First, avoid those communication/responsibility stoppers (aka Roadblocks) already discussed: nagging, ordering, threatening, moralizing, lecturing, using sarcasm, criticizing/judging, and giving advice/solutions.

And secondly, avoid these two additional blockers:[13] Reassurance and Distractions.

Blocker	Example
Reassuring him that everything will be all right	"You're a great player! What does that coach know, anyway?" *or* "Don't worry about it. There's always next season."
Distracting him/telling him to forget about it	"Tell you what, son. We'll go on a fishing trip this weekend and have lots of fun."

The hardest to avoid are the ones we heard as children: usually the very ones we presently use the most. Instead, we can put his feelings into words when *that* speaker sounds louder.

"I can hear how disappointed you are."

Then, when the *idea*-speaker becomes the louder one, we can paraphrase his words. "Sounds like you've decided to...."

Another extremely important process is taking place at this same time, but we must be watchful, or we'll miss it. While we're helping our child defuse his feelings so that he's able to move into addressing and solving his problem, we can be *learning about our child*.

Through avoiding the communication/feeling blockers, we're able to listen and observe our child, thus learning how he is processing the situation. This is Step 5 of the lesson plan. As we learn how our child is processing a particular situation, we're helped in knowing what to say next. Here's a possible scenario:

Disappointment of a Lifetime

Child: I *have* to be on the A team.

(Do you hear the emotion? Put it into words.)

Parent: "It's really hard to accept it when you don't get on the team you wanted the most."

Child: "Yeah and they picked that new kid. I play better than him."

Parent: "Very maddening, I'd say."

Child: "Yeah, and I'm really, really mad at all of them."

(Provide Wait Time, maybe even a minute or more. You're making space for him to think.)

Child: "Anyway, I've *got* to play soccer even if it's on that dumb B team."

Parent: "You think you may want to play on the B team?"

(Paraphrase to check your understanding of what he said.)

Child: "NO, I don't *want* to play on the B team. It's the *only* way I can play."

Parent: "You'd rather play on the B team than not play all. Is that what you mean?"

Child: "I guess so."

(Wait Time again)

Child: "All my friends made the A team, and now they'll think I'm a loser 'cause I have to play on the B team."

(You know this isn't true but avoid reassuring and distracting. Instead, continue putting his feelings into words or paraphrasing his ideas as appropriate. This is how you help him most, by teaching him a constructive process for dealing with disappointment.)

Parent: "You're worried about what your friends will think."

If you are listening and watching carefully, you'll be learning a great deal about his growing ability to handle his feelings of frustration and anger. You will learn the kinds of responses that help him move through his feelings and those that are counterproductive for this particular child. You'll be learning when to allow silence for him to think and whether to put his feelings or his ideas into words. Every child handles anger differently, and our job as parents is to guide and support while avoiding all those triggers on that Communication and Responsibility blocks list.

During this ongoing conversation, your son may wall up in his room, may come out periodically to say something else or may not mention it again. The important point is for him to know you're there if he wants to talk to you. A couple of days later, if he hasn't told you, you might ask him what he has decided to do.

His response may well be an anger tinged: "I've got to play on the B team."

That's okay. Over time, other anger may surface. Your job is to put his feeling or ideas into words, as appropriate, in order to allow him to deal with the disappointment as he plays with team members he sees as less skilled than he is.

And the hardest part of this process is sticking to merely paraphrasing and putting feelings into words. We desperately want to take away their hurt and save our children from it, but life includes hurts and disappointments. Don't we want to teach them how to handle those instead of running away from them? They only get larger as they get older.

He'll work it through because he has *you* on his team. Isn't it interesting that you haven't *told* him anything? You haven't judged his behavior and you haven't blamed him or the coach.

You have, however, guided and encouraged him by recognizing his feelings and allowing him to *have* those feelings. You did this by showing your understanding through paraphrasing his ideas and allowing time for him to think while you took the time and interest to sit nearby and just listen.

In addition, and very, very importantly, you have modeled a process for dealing with disappointment. He will eventually be equipped to follow this process on his own because you have *shown* him how to do it.

This is not to say you never give information or ask questions or share your experiences. All of these may be appropriate *later* when strong negative feelings are not predominating. If you had a similar disappointment when you were a kid, by all means tell your story, *but* timing is the key to helping your child. You don't want to change the topic from him to you, which telling your story would do, and you don't want to give the message that he will get over it just as you did. Rather, you want to tell your story at such a time that it expresses your empathy and understanding of *his* situation.

This lesson plan has been concentrating on the teaching steps of modeling and guiding and encouraging. It sounds so easy when you read the example, but when you start to limit yourself to putting feelings into words and paraphrasing ideas, you will probably feel absolutely foolish. You'll think nothing is happening, but you will be amazed at how your child is able to solve his problem himself when you give him the space and support described here.

Later, when he does play with the B Team, you can continue giving encouragement by putting his strengths into words. As brought out in a previous chapter, the most successful way to encourage a child is to describe a *specific* and *positive* observation you made and to name the strength you observed.

An example might be, "I saw that even though you were extremely disappointed at not getting on the A team, you're giving your all to the B team by going to every practice and game. I'd call that strong sportsmanship. I'm proud of you."

Most parents ask "Why not tell him his negative behavior? How else will he learn to improve and not to be so sulky or stormy?" The answer, again, is that by not mentioning negative behavior during the time he's having highly negative feelings, and instead, putting his feelings and ideas into words, and verbalizing our positive observations, parents help children and adolescents recognize their positive actions and rebuild self-esteem.

Whenever we parents use one of those communication blocking statements, we create a need for our child *either* to defend himself or to give up. In both instances, we have built a roadblock in our child's path to moving through his feelings and into creating ideas of what he'll do next. If a particular negative behavior is forming a pattern, it does need to be addressed, with an I-Message, but at a separate and calmer time.)

When I first learned about responding to an upset or even a hostile child by merely recognizing and naming the feelings, paraphrasing the words, and concentrating on the positive, I honestly thought it was bunk. The only reason I even gave it a chance was that the research was so convincing, and I am a big fan of *good* research.

When I started to eliminate the communication and responsibility-blockers, I not only had a fifteen-year-old, but also a thirteen-year-old, and an eleven-year-old, and I really found it difficult to discipline my responses. Every comment that immediately came to mind was on the "Do not say" list, so I was constantly thinking, "What *do* I say?"

That alone slowed me down and allowed time for me to think before I spoke. Now, these thirty-plus years of experience later–years as a teacher, a parent, and a grandparent–I've experienced over and over the almost miraculous effectiveness of this process for teaching children how to become responsible for their feelings, choices, and actions.

The second part of teaching our children how to deal with disappointment is teaching them how to solve a problem. Of course, we can solve the problems for our kids but when we do that, we prevent them from experiencing the gradual process of learning how to become responsible for solving their own problems. And when we begin while our child is very young, as with the "Who feeds the dog?" scenario, we can teach our child how to engage in problem-solving while we guide and coach as he practices the skills.

Such a process can be used with many different types of problems. The most common one we all encounter arises within interpersonal relationships.

Teach Them How to Solve Problems

Your second grader has just gotten off the bus and you know immediately that she is really upset. She runs up to you, and between sobs tells you how her best friend was mean to her all day, not sitting with her at lunch and then at recess, whispering to another girl about her and laughing.

Your heart is breaking. You want to make her pain go away, and you know there will be many more such painful experiences as she grows up. You can tell her to forget it and reassure her that tomorrow her friend will be her friend again which is probably true. You can call the other girl's mom and enlist her in helping the girls to get along. You can call the school and ask the teacher to investigate the situation. *Or,* you can use this experience to teach your daughter how to handle a problem.

Back to the lesson plan process. The learning objective has just been stated, "With guidance, Melanie will be able to make a plan for solving a problem with her friend and carry it through," but this time you are *not* going to share this objective with your child. Because she is little and is hurting, you're going to launch into the lesson by guiding and encouraging her.

Her immediate need is to know that you care and that you understand her feelings. She needs encouragement, and, as in the previous case, she needs the kind of encouragement that allows her to *feel* the pain and move through it. It bears repeating to say that this happens when Mom and Dad put the feelings into words and then listen as she talks or hold her while she cries.

RESPONSIBLE KIDS: 6 STEPS TO CREATING THEM IN AN IRRESPONSIBLE WORLD

> **I Don't Ever Want to Be Her Friend Again.**
>
> **Child** running up to you in tears: "Tanja…. and then she…and they laughed at me."
> **Parent**: "Oh Honey, I can see how hurt you feel."
> **Child**: "Yes, she hurt my feelings. I don't want her for a friend ever again!"
> **Parent**: "Sounds like you're mad too—both hurt and mad."
> **Child**: "I hate her!"
> **Parent**: "It's so hard when your best friend isn't nice to you."
> **Child**: "I'm going to do the same thing to her tomorrow. Then she'll know how it feels."
> **Parent**: "Tanja hurt you, now you feel like getting back at her."

Please, reread the interchange above. Note what was on the tip of *your* tongue each time your daughter spoke. Most likely, each of your responses would fall into the conversation/feeling/responsibility blocker statements below:

Blocker	Example
Reassuring	"By next week you'll be best friends again." (*This is not support and encouragement because it may not be true and it says, "I don't take your feelings seriously."*)
Distracting	"I know just how to make you feel better. Come in and we'll have some ice cream." (*This encourages a child to bury her feelings rather than recognizing and dealing with them.*)
Giving Advice	"Just call her on the phone, Honey. Friends are always having fights."
Moralizing	"Now, Sweetie, being mean to someone is never the answer."

| Criticizing/judging | "They were being mean little girls, and you're not a mean little girl." |

These familiar types of responses were the common ones most of us heard growing up. It's only natural that we say them too, but today we know that people work through their feelings more successfully when someone responds with empathy instead of with any of the familiar blocker statements.

Once your daughter's feeling a little better, she'll be ready to begin learning, and you can start the lesson. Be prepared for her to continue expressing her feelings as you discuss the issue, and when she does, just respond with empathy by again putting her feelings into words, thus helping her to feel your ongoing understanding. Continue to help her sort out her own feelings by listening carefully enough to recognize whether feelings or words are stronger and alternating back and forth as needed between putting her feelings into words and paraphrasing what she says.

When the problem-solving lesson begins, you can ask your child to put the problem into a sentence. Help her to do this because it is essential to clarify the issue. Avoid, at all costs, doing this for her. Instead, ask her questions to lead her, but let the wording be her own. As you listen to her attempts to put the problem into her own words, you'll be learning about how she's processing the situation and what she's thinking which is an essential part of the lesson plan for the teacher. When your daughter has a clear wording of the problem, write it at the top of a piece of paper:

Problem: **My best friend was mean to me and got other kids to be mean to me. I want her to know she hurt my feelings and say she's sorry.**

Continue by brainstorming a few ideas, asking if she would like to give the first idea. Offer your idea when appropriate, and model non-judgment of *any* ideas. Using the paper on which you wrote out the problem, make a list of possible solutions. Remember, no judgment of any idea no matter how crazy it may sound to you:

1. Call Tanya's mother and tell her how mean Tanya was. (This may seem positive to a young child. *Later,* as you examine the ideas to choose one, you can ask a question such as "Do you think Tanya would really mean it if her mother *made* her say she was sorry?" and then you can discuss it.)
2. Call Tanya and ask if she can get together and talk about what happened at school. (At this young age, a good idea is to include a parent of each girl in the meeting to model empathy and give information as needed.)
3. Tell Ms. Smart, (the school counselor) and have her talk with Tanya and me together. (This is a good idea if you and Tanya's parent feel a bit shaky about guiding the girls in such a discussion.)

Now discuss each idea together, and you guide her in choosing an appropriate action by asking questions for her consideration and by adding some information. Choose one idea from the list to begin the process.

You may offer your thoughts about the one you would start with, but allow your child to make the final decision, keeping in mind that each idea *must not* be hurtful or destructive.

During your problem-solving discussion, be sure to avoid the "blockers" and instead, periodically identify specific positive things your child is saying and doing.

Some examples might be, "You know, Honey, I see that you're taking time to try and solve a problem with your friend, and I call that being (a patient friend, a caring friend…" or any other specific you're observing).

Once you and your daughter have decided which idea to carry out, you can begin. And don't worry because you are going to be right there to guide and support your little girl when she makes the phone call, and at the meeting, too, if that's what everyone involved decides. P. S.

Please remember the last step in every lesson plan: "repeat everything as often as it takes, never giving up."

~ ~ ~ ~

"Yes," over and over again, "yes;" good parenting takes an exorbitant amount of time. We could handle the whole thing much faster ourselves; we could call Tanya's mother and between the two of us, we could probably take care of the issue. Tanya's mother could tell you your daughter called her daughter a bad name the day before, and that she was just reacting to that, and then you both could make the girls apologize to each other, and then they'd probably be friends again…*but* let's remind ourselves of the main goal in this situation.

Is it to have the child and her friend patch up their quarrel? No.

The main goal is to teach our child a problem-solving process to use throughout life. If additional issues had been involved, they would surface during the girls' discussion, and the girls would have discovered it together; a much deeper learning experience than occurs from being told what the issue is and how to solve it, thus depriving the children of guided practice in actually doing it.

An appropriate comparison might be to think of any life skill and how we learn to become good at. Take learning to play a musical instrument, or to play soccer, or to swim, make a cake, ride a bike. A book or a person can give information, but for us to become skillful, we must practice, practice, practice with the support and diligent guidance of our teacher/parent/coach.

This method can be used for solving *all types* of problems and for doing so at any age. The beauty of this method expresses itself through the discussions we're having with our child. When we engage in problem-solving and truly listen to the feelings and ideas of the other person, we learn about that person on a deep level. When it comes to our children, the deeper our understanding of them, the better parent we can become. When we teach our children the *process* of listening and solving problems with another, we equip them with essential life skills.

~ ~ ~ ~

"But, Dad, *all* my friends' parents are buying them a car for their sixteenth birthday."

If you have just heard this statement from your soon-to-be sixteen-year-old, you know you've got work ahead of you. To begin turning things around, you might use this answer, careful to avoid all the communication/feeling stoppers.

"Tell me more." *Yes, I am for real.* Let your son or daughter go on and on, until you've heard them out. Now they're ready for information from you:

> **Parent**: I can see how much you'd like to have a car, and I'm willing to help you achieve your dream. Your Mom and I aren't willing to buy you a car (*giving your boundaries*), but we'll help you save for one. (*Be prepared for an outburst that won't be pretty.*)
>
> **Teen**: "You don't even care that I'll be the only girl in school without a car. You don't understand anything! I knew I couldn't depend on you!" She shouts as she storms out, probably to her room from where you hear the bang of her slamming door.

DO NOT SAY IT! Avoid reacting with "Young Lady, that kind of behavior will get you grounded," or anything equally threatening. Instead, start fleshing out the lesson plan. It's very, very important to stay on the subject of *this* conflict and, if needed, to deal later with any other ones. You are about to teach another lesson on solving problems but not until she has had time to calm down and is ready to make a plan.

This time the learning objective is that your daughter will be able to make a plan for how she can buy her own car. And again, a lot of discussion will be involved because you'll be doing all the things an effective parent/teacher does; put feelings and ideas into words, guide, support, and give some information as your daughter makes a plan to solve her problem.

During these problem-solving sessions, as much as you want to give information, and you will provide *some,* the most important input you can provide is your guidance and encouragement through your continual listening.

Because this is a long plan, you will need to listen to feelings by identifying them and listen to ideas by paraphrasing often to check your understanding and to help your daughter clarify her own thinking.

Remember to identify specific strengths you see her using, for example, "I know this is time consuming and difficult, and I see you're taking the time to go through this process anyway. I'd say that show's strong self-discipline, a trait necessary to be a safe driver."

Again, you guide with the same process you did when she was in second grade. Hopefully, you started teaching her then, or earlier, so that by now it's second nature for her. Even if this is the case, she still needs you to guide, to offer information and ask questions, encourage when she gets discouraged, and to help her retackle the issue if her initial ideas for solving the problem don't pan out. Repeat everything as often as it takes. It will be worth it!

Some ideas that might be offered during the brainstorming step could include the following, and of course, included with no judgment given:

1. Parents loan the money, and the teen pays it back from a part time job over a two-year period.
2. Teen finds a part time job and saves money for one year and parents match the amount at that time.
3. As long as the teen maintains Dean's List standing, the parents will pay for a car.

Once the list is complete, and the discussion begins, you'll be amazed at the creative ways in which you find yourselves combining ideas from the original list and even creating probable solutions neither of you would have thought of on your own.

Such a process not only teaches children how to solve their problems, but also gives them the experience of achieving something valuable for themselves, an accomplishment that builds self-confidence and healthy independence. Because we parents are guiding them throughout, we're able to provide the encouragement and empathy they need in order to work through what is often a long and laborious period of time.

Another perfect topic for problem-solving arises with "allowances." Kids want them, and parents usually give them without much thought. However, then parents often experience a huge dilemma when it comes to knowing when to give kids what they ask for and when to expect them to buy it for themselves–or at least contribute to its purchase.

Ah ha! A most productive time for a lesson plan. If we expect our kids to become responsible spenders and savers, we need to take the time to teach them *how* to become financially responsible. Giving them each an allowance creates a strong learning activity.

Before creating the learning objective, we need to clarify *for ourselves* the purpose of an allowance. Most people believe it is something we give our children for doing their household jobs. With that in mind, I suggest reviewing Step 2, "Expect Nothing from Them, or Teach Them How to Take Part in Life Outside Themselves."

We learned that the purpose behind our children having household responsibilities is to contribute to family life. If we parents *pay* our kids for those jobs, then the message of being a contributing family member gets all muddied up. So how do they earn money when they're not old enough to hold a job?

They don't earn it. Parents give allowances to children. "Why?" you may ask.

The answer is so we can teach the lessons of how to become a responsible spender and saver, thus solving the problem of how to handle their money. This is the sole reason for giving children an allowance.

Parents again create a lesson plan, beginning this time with step #1, giving information. We explain that the purpose of an allowance is to let children experience solving the problem of how they will divide their money into the big three categories: "Spending," "Saving," and "Donating" Yes, "Donating" is an important bucket because they're learning how to become a responsible part of the larger community. They'll probably think this is wrong and let you know that their friends get paid for doing jobs at home and that that's the real purpose of an allowance. We, however, calmly respond, "In our family, we all do jobs around the house because we want to help each other. You get an allowance for a different reason."

Together, everyone can make a list of the types of things the children would be expected to buy for themselves. Kindergarteners and first graders might buy such things as candy, gum, balloons; third graders might also buy candy, gum, etc. and also pay for library fines; high schoolers might still have the candy, etc., and also pay for lost or damaged textbooks. Collaborative decisions are based on the children's ages, needs, and capabilities.

In the category of "Donating," the parent can give information about various causes and charities and each child can choose a favorite. Parents can provide information about banks, savings accounts, investing, etc. To teach children about various causes and ways to save and/or invest their money, parents can create learning activities such as internet searches, reading and discussing books, field trips, etc.

The problem-solving activity for this lesson is creating a budget. The problem might be stated as a question: "How much will I put into each area?" Brainstorming ensues followed by discussion and finally making choices.

Lastly, the child tries her choices, and a couple of weeks later revises *or* continues with her original list.

What happens when the kids run out of money before they run out of things to buy? And they will. *They go without.* At first a sad lesson, and you will no doubt be nagged nearly to death, maybe you'll even feel guilty. Comfort yourself with the knowledge that the children have experienced only *part* of the lesson plan and it's now time to move on to the next part.

Avoiding the communication/feeling stoppers, it is back to the guide and encourage stage, as you allow them to experience the natural consequences of their decisions. They will move through their disappointments and become ready once again to go back to the problem-solving board to make a plan for how to avoid such a catastrophe in the future.

We all know they will not completely avoid such a catastrophe again, but the important part of the lesson right now is the process. A process that's providing children with two life skills: solving a problem and handling money responsibly. It is much less painful to be unable to buy a bag of candy or a book than it will be to have a car or home repossessed! Let them learn the lesson early in life while we can be a "safety net" of sorts.

Reminder: be sure to review the lesson plan for your role in this process, especially the guide and support part of the plan.

~ ~ ~ ~

Not only is it important for us to teach our children the skills of problem-solving in the context of our home, but it's also essential for us to carry this teaching over into the context of school.

When children begin school, parents join an especially important team to promote learning how to become responsible. The team consists of the teacher, the parents, *and* the student. Sound familiar? I mentioned it earlier.

That's right; the child is an essential member of the team and participates in the parent-teacher-student conferences. If our goal is to help our children become responsible for their *own* learning and behavior in school, they have to practice by taking part in creating solutions for the inevitable problems that arise. Being a team member is the *learning activity* and all the other parts of the lesson plan make up this ongoing *learning experience*. I, unfortunately, didn't learn the importance of this teamwork lesson until, as a relatively inexperienced high school teacher, I experienced a most uncomfortable situation that created negative feelings for all of us–the mother, the student, and me. Let me explain.

My sophomores had completed their research papers; a process that had been carried out over several weeks' time and in a step-by-step process. At each step, I had given students individual feedback and written instructions for their next step. Meanwhile, Adam was not doing his work in a timely manner, nor was he completing the editing I suggested in my feedback to him. I met with him individually, sent home a progress report (this was before parents were connected to the internet) to let his parents know what the problems were, and continued to work with him individually as well as in class.

Adam returned the signed progress report, and I heard no more from his parents. Adam continued to fall behind despite my feedback. He turned in his final research paper, and I scored it according to the rubric students had been given. Adam scored 75%, a D in our school system.

When the quarter grades came out, Adam's mother called me in a panic, asking for a meeting to find out why Adam's quarter grade was so low. She was terribly upset because Adam had told her he had to write "all these papers" and that he'd had "no idea how to do them or even when they were due."

I agreed we needed to talk, and I also realized Adam was feeling trapped and thus trying desperately to protect himself with lies. Yes, he created the situation, but I reminded myself, he is learning to become responsible for his behavior. I asked her to invite Adam to the meeting too. Of course, Adam declined the invitation. In a burst of insight, I explained that we couldn't meet unless he participated because he needed to explain his problems for us to understand his needs.

We met. Adam's mom explained what Adam had told her, and every so often Adam would sheepishly edit something she said. When the story of how I had failed Adam was finished, I asked Adam if he wanted to add anything–I even gave him a lead by asking if he wanted to tell his mom about the directions for the paper. Adam stared down at the floor and remained silent.

I gave her a folder containing copies of his work with my ongoing feedback and directions for next steps. Needless to say, all the facts came out, even the fact that Adam had intercepted the progress report, and his mom was mortified. Adam wasn't very comfortable either. I too felt bad because I didn't enjoy putting his mother in an embarrassing situation, and I did not enjoy exposing the lies Adam told.

Even though in today's school world, the internet gives parents ongoing information which might prevent a parent's shock, the point of the story is that this traditional type of parent-teacher meeting is all too often a "gotcha session" and the victim is either the teacher–which this one started out to be–or the student–which this one turned out to be. It's a power struggle with winners and losers. Adam was the loser and as such left the meeting with feelings of failure and possibly of shame. In a power struggle, no one *wins*. I now know that *none* of this had to happen.

We all could have been winners. If Adam's experience from the time he started school had been that when there's a problem, he is able to take part in finding a solution, he would have been more likely to believe in his own ability to tackle the problem rather than to run from it. He might have asked for a team meeting.

If we are to teach our children to become responsible, we must provide the situations for them to practice taking on responsibility for problem-solving, especially when they're young. That way we're still there to guide, support, and offer information in the process of parenting and teaching.

Thinking of an effective lesson plan, let's consider the question of what an effective learning objective would be for a team conference. In the example that I just shared, we didn't have a written objective, but sadly, we ended up with the following *unwritten* one: "Adam will admit his lies and apologize."

How humiliating for Adam. Clearly a negative. How much more empowering *this* would have been: "Adam will demonstrate the ability to brainstorm ways to help avoid putting off his work until the last minute and put selected ideas into practice with the next assignment."

If we had been working as a team from the beginning, this second objective could have been put into practice as teacher and parents guided and encouraged. Everyone would have been a winner.

A Word of Warning:

Teaching a problem-solving process to our children can interfere with our own "need to be needed." As our children become more and more successful at solving their problems, they consult us less frequently, and we may find ourselves feeling left out or not needed.

As our children gain confidence in solving their problems, they will expect us to avoid what they see as interference. As a parent, I failed to recognize my own need to be needed and consequently almost fell into the trap of solving a problem for my middle daughter–a problem she was capable of handling on her own.

During her senior year, she was directing a school play, and the students practiced after school in the auditorium. One morning, the assistant principal "accosted" my daughter in the hall, blaming her for a mess that had been left in the auditorium after a practice session.

She came home and burst into tears, "…and he wouldn't even let me explain that the principal had given me permission to leave the scenery drawings on the floor."

Instantly, my motherly instincts went into overdrive, and I was halfway out the door before she was able to stop me from going to the school at that very moment to confront that assistant principle and defend my daughter.

She told me I was to stay out of it, that she would handle it the next day. And she did. Momentarily I felt discarded–I had to have a little talk with myself to appreciate the situation for what it *really* was. She still needed me, but on a different level. She no longer needed me to help her solve the problem; she needed me to listen and understand her feelings.

I took a step back from my own insecure feelings and realized my parenting was paying off. She was becoming successfully independent– and isn't that the point we want our children to reach by the time they're seniors? I still felt a bit sad at the thought of my little girl being almost grown up, but I also felt great pride and a sense of confidence that she was ready to handle going away to college the next fall.

Because of my confidence in Kristin's readiness to begin responsible independence, I was in for a shock that fall when we attended her college orientation day. As the Dean of Students was explaining a bit about campus life and answering parent questions, the tension began to rise, and with each question he answered, parent anxiety mounted until parents were bursting out with angry comments.

"What do you mean you don't notify us if our daughter is skipping classes or failing a course!"

"I'm paying the bills here and I can't see my son's grades unless he shows them to me?"

"No one checks to make sure my daughter is safely checked into the dorm at night?"

These types of fears were being shouted at the Dean from all around the room. That was thirty years ago and guess what? It's still going on!

My middle daughter and her oldest experienced these same parental fears and angry demands during Syd's college orientation day.

The reality is that when our children go off to college, they are on their own. That bears repeating. **They are on their own**.

Either we have taught them the skills needed for successful responsible independence, or we haven't. Either we have created a close and trusting relationship with them, or we have not. Beginning early to teach our children how to deal with their disappointments and problems in responsible ways allows them opportunities to practice, to make mistakes, and to cope with any uncomfortable consequences. This process is carried out when we're right there to guide, model, give information, and encouragement, and *never giving up*.

By the time they are seventeen or eighteen and leaving for college, we want them to be equipped with the life skills they need to be ready for the responsibilities they will have, right?

TOOLS #5

Two New Communication/Responsibility-Blockers to Avoid

Blocker | **Example**
Reassuring: | "Everything will be fine."
 | "Next week you'll forget all about it."

Distracting: | "Forget about it and let's play that X Box game."

List of Communication/Responsibility-Blockers so far

Ordering

Warning

Using Sarcasm

Criticizing/Judging

Lecturing

Reminding/Nagging

Giving Advice (solving the problem for your child)

Moralizing

Reassuring

Distracting

Communication/Responsibility-Building Skills That Focus Us Away from the Blockers

I-Messages
Paraphrasing words and ideas
Putting feelings into words

These skills help us in our efforts to avoid the communication and responsibility-blockers. Most importantly, when we carry on conversations using I-Messages, naming our child's feelings, and checking our understanding of what our child is saying, we are **building our relationship** and **modeling** how to interact in all healthy relationships.

Gentle Reminder About Listening to the Louder Speaker: Feelings or Words

When we state our expectation, even in an I-Message, we may well be met with anger, denial, resistance, or any other negative response. That's the time to name that feeling we are hearing, and we continue to recognize those feelings until our child's *feelings*-speaker is turned down.

At that point, we can try again to speak our expectations. What happens then, is that the *feelings*-speaker will probably get loud again, and we're back to having to recognize feelings. This dance can go on for some time, as we switch back and forth in order to reach a place where we and our child can problem-solve the issue.

Problem-Solving

Write out the problem in as few words as possible, and then brainstorm ideas for solving it. Remember, at this stage, all ideas are written down without any criticism or judgment. When your list is complete, discuss each idea, eliminating the ones you think won't work. Then choose one of the remaining ideas to try. After a few days, review together to assess how that choice is working. If either of you is unhappy with it, try another idea from that list.

STEP 6

SIXTH STEP TO CREATING *IRRESPONSIBLE* KIDS

Expect Obedience

"When I was a kid, I was expected to follow the rules or else!"

"Hey, when I was growing up, I got punished plenty and even spanked when I needed it, and I don't have any responsibility issues."

"Punishing kids when they need it gets them ready for the real world. If you speed, you get fined; if you don't do your job, you get fired. That's reality."

SIXTH STEP TO CREATING *RESPONSIBLE* KIDS

Teach Them How to Work Through a Power Struggle

Understanding Our Role in The Power Struggle

Why do we want our kids to obey the rules? No seriously, stay with me. What are the reasons kids need to follow the rules and expectations?

- To avoid getting punished
- To be safer
- To stay out of trouble
- Because the rules are just and necessary for the well-being of everyone

Our answer is probably "yes" to all the above and we might even think of additional reasons. Throughout this book, you have read that when we use any of the relationship blockers: ordering, warning, sarcasm, criticizing or judging, lecturing/reminding/nagging, giving advice (aka solving the problem for your child), moralizing, reassuring, or distracting, we start a power struggle with our kids.

We no doubt all agree we want our kids to follow rules because they see those rules as just and fair and reasonable even when they disagree with them. How do we get our kids to that point? That is the question.

Children want what they want, and they truly don't understand why they cannot have it. Immediately if not sooner. To get what they want, they usually learn power struggle (fighting) behavior early: pleading, cajoling, promising, and finally, if none of the preceding has worked, yelling, and/or sulking.

They apprentice in childhood to an older sibling or a TV show actor, become adept by third grade, and are masters by 5th grade. Some even carry these behaviors into adulthood where they model them for their own children.

When we tell children what they can and cannot do, give them few or no choices, and do not engage with them in the give and take of a decision-making process, we are depriving them of the practice time to learn *how* to engage in responsible decision-making behavior.

We are also depriving them of *another* essential part of the lesson–our modeling of how to discuss, disagree, and even argue, in a caring, responsible manner.

I didn't begin to learn *any* of these skills until my oldest daughter was fifteen, and at first, she did not like my change one bit. The whole process was foreign to her, especially the new language I was using.

In one of her volcanic eruptions, she screamed at me, "Why don't you just tell me what to do like you used to? Then I know how to fight back."

That was a very revealing moment! It suddenly hit me. Did I really want to be creating a perfect setting for teenage power struggles? Or did I want to be teaching my child how to think for herself in order to solve problems?

Working Through the Power Struggle

"Problem-solving skills are dumb," announced Carson, a boy in my Freshman English class. "Everybody knows the person who yells the loudest gets what he wants."

Knowing his father, a highly successful attorney and a school board member in our town, I understood why Carson believed that was true. I also knew most people were intimidated by his dad; thus, he *did* get what he wanted.

The long-term outcome, though, was that most people *avoided* him.

We learn early in life that power struggles are inevitable. We have only to observe a couple of toddlers who are just learning to talk:

> **Mike** toddles over to Jake, snatches his toy and scoots away with it.
> **Jake** screams "I had it first," and runs after Mike to get it back.
> *(He may also hit Mike and yell, "bad boy." Or, when Mike grabs his toy, Jake may just sit down and cry.)*

Okay, but don't we want our kids to be able to stick up for themselves? You bet we do, but the truth is that most of our interactions don't require us to use the tactics of fight or flight–it's just that those are the tactics we have learned through observation and experience.

There are alternatives, alternatives aimed at maintaining and building our relationships with others (friend to friend, parent to child, sibling to sibling, colleague to colleague, boss to employee, neighbor to neighbor, etc.) These alternatives allow us to stick up for ourselves in the process.

All the skills discussed in the previous sections of this handbook are directed at teaching our kids the skills for working through a power struggle instead of fighting. And when we parents model those skills and engage our children in using them, we're teaching them how to deal with conflict in responsible, caring ways; ways that promote positive relationships and still maintain individual integrity. When we are teaching them how to do things for themselves, how to take part in life outside themselves, how to make healthy choices, how to deal with disappointment and solve problems, and how to deal with uncomfortable consequences, we're also teaching them how to engage in problem-solving rather than in starting or furthering a power struggle.

In a power struggle, the goal is winning; therefore, someone must lose. When one person in a relationship becomes a loser because of the actions of the other, the relationship often becomes damaged (hard feelings, eroded trust, distance). When this happens repeatedly over time, the damage to the relationship can become so severe that the people live in constant conflict or avoid each other completely.

Everything in our culture shows us how to get entangled in conflict; "fight or flight" with the predominance being on "fight"– television shows, election campaigns, disgruntled store clerks, family members, friends, and even educators. The major problem in such power struggles is that all the participants are trying to force one another to change instead of taking a part in the responsibility for problem-solving the conflict.

Remember the boys in Chapter 1? Let's loop back and re-examine that home scene:

The Morning Scramble

"Steve, Sam, Time to get up."

(You hurry back to getting yourself dressed for work, and about five minutes later realize you've heard no movement from the bedroom.)

"Come on boys. You've got thirty minutes before the bus comes."

(No response. You go in and shake them gently, pulling off the covers.)

"Boys, you have to have time for breakfast."

(You vaguely feel your jaw tightening.)

"Ya, ya, I'll be right there," Steve mumbles as he pulls the sheet back up and over his head.

"Get up right this minute!"

(And now your jaw is aching.)

RESPONSIBLE KIDS: 6 STEPS TO CREATING THEM IN AN IRRESPONSIBLE WORLD

And now it's so late, that by the time they do get up and, with your constant nagging, have gathered all their school stuff (you hope) together, you end up driving them to school yet again.

This scene is a typical power struggle between parents and children, and as such it's a "game," but a game that's no fun, especially for you. It's so common in all aspects of our lives that the board on which the game is played was given a name by Stephen Karpman: The Drama Triangle.[14]

This triangle is an inverted pyramid with three positions, and the players take turns playing in each position.

The top right position is "Rescuer" (always shown with a capital letter to distinguish it from true help). Very often one or both parents assume this position by going too far in helping. We do the tasks our kids are totally capable of doing for themselves. We make decisions our children are developmentally ready to make for themselves. We solve their problems for them. We don't carry through on consequences.

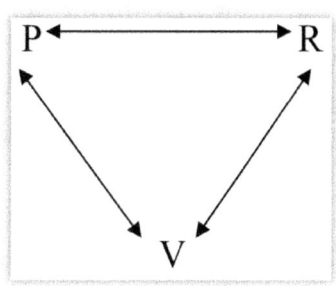

Once we assume this role, we have certain expectations of those we are rescuing. If our kids don't reciprocate, like do what we've told them to do such as get up on time, remember their school materials, get to the bus in time, we end up feeling exhausted, frazzled, and exploited. In other words, we feel victimized.

When this happens, we have moved to the position of Victim at the bottom point of the triangle. In Victim position we can withdraw, give up, sulk–any of the flight tactics–in our attempt to force our kids to do what we've told them to do. Although some people stay stuck in Victim position, most of us don't like it here, so we jump up to Persecutor position where we punish and use the responsibility/communication blocker statements (fight) as we continue our attempts to force our kids to do as they're told.

Because this is not a game of solitaire, our kids are also moving from position to position. As soon as we move into Persecutor position, our kids take a turn in the Victim position. And they don't like it any better than we did, so they usually move up to Persecutor position.

Now both parents and children are *together* in Persecutor position and a *really* good fight ensues. Kids can be even better than parents at this position. They pretend not to hear us, they yell at us to get off their backs, they tell us we're "mean" or "the worst parents ever," they hole up in their rooms, and refuse to talk. We've all been there with our kids and when *we* were kids, we were there with *our* parents.

If everyone stays inside the Triangle, the conflict continues to go round and round, each player fighting to get his own way until someone withdraws from open conflict in one of three ways:

1. She feels overpowered by the other–thus surrenders in **Victim** position.
2. She withdraws to make the other feel better–thus being in **Rescuer** position.
3. She continues for several hours or days to act hostile–thus staying stuck in **Persecutor** position.

Everyone feels exhausted and lousy about themselves and about one another. This drama separates people and can, over time, cause such deep negative feelings that people end the relationship. We all know of family members who refuse to talk to each other or best friends who have severed all ties.

The first time I saw this "game" drawn out and described, I recognized it immediately because my husband and I had been playing it with our oldest daughter *for fifteen years*. In our indescribable frustration at not being able to *control* her, we joined a parenting class hoping to learn more effective ways to control her behavior. I say we *recognize*d the game, but we weren't yet convinced that we were hopelessly trapped because our Boss strategies "worked" with our other two daughters. Obviously, we thought, the problem was not with ourselves, but rather with our "headstrong, stubborn, unmanageable" oldest child.

Over the next weeks, we were to learn a great deal about parenting in ways that would provide our children with opportunities to practice being responsible while we *guided* rather than *bossed*.

Through that process, we learned how to extricate ourselves, and eventually our children, from the Drama Triangle. We learned how to recognize the signs for when we had jumped back in, and we learned how to begin using the skills for teaching our children a process for becoming responsible for problem-solving rather than for merely doing as they were told.

We had been parenting in the only way we knew; the Boss way, and our well-intentioned insistence on the Boss way had been destroying our relationship with our oldest. We came to realize that the problem was not with our independent, freethinking, creative child, but, rather, with ourselves.

The path out of this destructive game is built through using the skills discussed throughout this handbook. Let's return to the "Morning Scramble" example. Who is taking the responsibility for the children being on time for school? Who is taking the responsibility for the children remembering all their materials?

Right, the parent is the Rescuer in this scene and thus is taking on a responsibility that belongs to the children. Eventually the parent feels frustrated and moves into the Victim position; then moves directly into Persecutor position by giving an order: "Get up right this minute!"

The parent may jump back and forth, first to Rescuer position as she continues to remind and then to Persecutor as the reminding becomes nagging and threatening. Then, after all this conflict, the parent continues the power struggle from Rescue position by driving the children to school! As she drives away, realizing she is late for work, what Drama Triangle position do you think she's in?

Because everyone was in the Drama Triangle, the children learned nothing about how to take responsibility for getting themselves up, about ways to remember their own materials, and about how to deal with the consequences of their decision not to get up on time for school. Because they missed out on learning all these things, they are also missing out on the gradual learning of how their decisions impact others–either to the other's benefit like their parent gets to work on time–or to the other's detriment, like their parent is late for work.

So how do we get out of this mess? The way out of the Drama Triangle is for one of the players to *quit*. And that is exactly what happened when the parents gave their children the gift of an alarm clock and explained the parameters of the activity for getting themselves up and out to school instead of having their parents do it for them.

Whenever we parents take *any* position in the Drama Triangle, we set up a probable conflict, and we deprive our children of the opportunity to practice how to carry out their own particular responsibility.

Even though the way out of the Drama Triangle begins with one person's using the relationship-building skills and avoiding the communication/feeling blockers, the others don't always follow, especially in the beginning. After all, this game is the one we have all been learning throughout our lives.

Going back to the scene in Step 5 where the teen expected her dad to buy her a car, the parent stayed out of the game. He did so by showing his desire to help his daughter achieve her dreams by problem-solving with her and making the parameters include her own responsibility in the project. No rescuing.

But just because Dad wasn't playing the game does not mean Daughter wasn't trying to play. She told him all her friends' parents were buying them a car (Victim), that he was unreasonable in not doing the same (Persecutor), and she went on and on about not wanting to make a plan, yelling sarcastically at her dad that he "always had to have a plan" (Persecutor).

How did the dad continue to avoid the Triangle? He *listened* to her feelings when they were louder than her words and *paraphrased* her words when they were louder than her feelings. He did that until she was ready to make a plan.

He "stuck up for himself" by setting his boundaries: "No, we will not buy you a car, but we'll help you brainstorm possible solutions" (make a plan). No matter how hard the daughter now continues to play the game, Dad remains outside by continuing to use the relationship-building skills.

Let's examine a conflict between a parent, determined to stay out of the Drama Triangle, and a teen still playing a strong game. Before we do, let's review four specific relationship-building skills. These skills are what we might term "soft" confrontation statements and are essential for staying out of the Drama Triangle during those times when our child is insisting he's a Victim by refusing to recognize that someone else *did not* cause his tribulations.

Skill	Example
Using a *What* question and avoiding the *Why* questions	"What are you doing now?" "What did you do?" "What do you plan to do now?"
Describing your child's behavior without judgment – just the facts. Can be combined with a What question effectively	"I noticed you decided to stay up past midnight playing your Xbox. Then today you came home and slept until dinner. What is your revised plan for doing your homework?"
Putting the child's feelings into words	"Sounds like you are feeling a lot of stress right now and that you don't have enough time just to veg out." (Later when child feels heard and understood, you'll return to a What question.)
Paraphrasing what you think your child is saying	"Are you saying you want to quit playing lacrosse?"

Let's now examine how one parent uses these skills along with avoiding the responsibility/communication blockers.

Eighth Grade Melissa did not get up this morning when her alarm rang, and according to parental parameters, she had to walk to school. She was late and received a Saturday detention.

Her mom walks in from work and the dishes are still in the sink and laundry unfolded, both Melissa's tasks. Mom finds Melissa moping in her room.

It's All Your Fault

"Everything okay?" Mom asks, checking feelings first.

"I got a Saturday detention (tone of **Victim** position), and it's all your fault," says Melissa, quickly switching to **Persecutor** position.

"What happened?" Mom asks, using a What question.

(At this point Mom is tired, discouraged, and probably tense. She really wants to respond with "If you'd gotten up when…" But this blame statement would put her right into the Drama Triangle and the power-struggle).

"You made me late for school because you wouldn't drive me," Melissa says, feeling like a **Victim**, but immediately jumping up to **Persecutor** position with a You-blaming statement. "There's no reason *you* couldn't drive me, so it's all your fault."

Mom identifies Melissa's feelings. "I can hear how angry you are." (*Emotions are louder than words so Mom identifies feelings*.)

"And now I can't go to Tatianna's sleepover on Friday," Melissa snarls, back in **Victim** position.

(Wait time— 3-5 seconds)

"Well, you know, I see this very differently," says Mom, giving information with an I-Message.

"You *always* see it differently, but that doesn't mean it *is* different." (*Hear those angry emotions.*)

> "I know you're very angry right now. And I'm sorry you have to give up a Saturday morning that you counted on being with your friends." (*Showing true empathy*).
>
> "You're not sorry at all. If you cared, you wouldn't let me be late for school," retorts Melissa from the **Victim** position.
>
> *Wait time (3-5 seconds)*

It may be that Melissa's feelings are so intense that Mom tables the discussion until a later time, or it may be that the daughter begins to feel defused because Mom has used no responsibility blockers and has thus stayed out of the Triangle. In either case the conversation continues either now or later as appropriate.

> "I know you're really upset about the detention, and I'd like to work with you to help you avoid another one (*Step #6, never giving up*). Of course, anything we work out has to be within the boundaries your dad and I laid out in the beginning when we explained your responsibility for getting yourself up and to school on time (*Step #1, giving information*). When you're ready, we can brainstorm a list of things you might do so that you're not late again." (*Invitation to solve this problem*)
>
> "What do you mean?" Melissa asks indignantly from **Victim** position.
>
> "Well, when your alarm went off this morning, what did you do?" Mom asks, staying with the What question.
>
> "Nothing. I shut it off."
>
> *(Wait time)*
>
> When Melissa doesn't answer, Mom asks, "Then what did you do?"
>
> "I tried to get up, but it was too cold." (**Victim**)

"So, you decided to stay in bed a while longer?" Mom asks so she understands.

"Yeah," Melissa says in the tone of "isn't that obvious?"

(Wait time)

"What! I *told* you, it was too cold," Melissa repeats, this time with attitude.

"Okay, so what you're saying is that you made a decision to stay in bed," says Mom, paraphrasing what her daughter just said in order to mirror it back to her.

"Yeah, but I had to because it was too cold to get up." (**Victim**)

"After you made that decision, what did you do?" Mom asks.

"I got up, but by then, I knew I was late."

"Then," says Mom (*being ever so careful to use conversational tone as she paraphrases for the purpose of holding up a mirror for her daughter to "see" what she has said*), "what I'm hearing is that because you made a choice to stay in bed, you missed the bus, had to walk to school, and got a Saturday detention for being late."

"Yeah, but *you* could've driven me," Melissa the **Persecutor** insists.

"You're right, Honey, I could have driven you. What does our plan say?"

(Wait time.)

Melissa, voice raised and kind of sing-songy, mimics, "It says I have to get myself up on time and if I miss the bus, I walk to school. But that's not fair." (**Victim**)

(Wait time)

"Parts of our plan are negotiable, but the parts where you get yourself up and to school on time—and I don't drive you—aren't negotiable. If you'd like to brainstorm some more ideas of how you'll do that, I'd be glad to work with you."

Then the problem-solving can begin, but not while emotion is high. When your daughter is calmer, begin by writing the problem at the top of the page for the brainstorming, "What can I do to get myself to school on time?"

This parent had become a master at using the relationship-building skills to stay out of the Drama Triangle, but of course her child was still stuck there. Children, and especially teens, will often play the Drama Triangle game even harder as they try to pull their parents back into what is familiar to them. Remember my experience when I first started to stay out of the Drama and my fifteen-year-old very angrily screamed, "Why don't you just yell and tell me what to do like you used to? Then I know how to fight back."

Because our daughter had experienced fifteen years of her parents modeling how to play the positions in the Drama Triangle, she had learned which position she would take next, thus what she would say next. When we weren't taking a position in the game, she literally didn't know which way to turn.

Taking our children into an unfamiliar way of interacting often leads to anxiety, thus making it even more important that we use the relationship-building skills, particularly the recognition of their feelings.

The anxiety isn't just in our kids either. When we first try out these unfamiliar ways of interacting, we feel artificial, and it takes a long time before the skills become "us." If we were not brought up with them, we may never master them; we'll just continue to become better and better at using them, like learning any new language as an adult.

Even after these thirty-five-plus years of practice, I still have times when I struggle to stay out of the Drama Triangle, and even times when I dive right into the thick of it.

Just the other day, after having listened to my youngest of eleven grandchildren carrying on in Victim position, I jumped right into Persecutor position with a "you statement."

"Your tone is very nasty right now," I pointed out sternly.

The good news is I immediately recognized it and extricated myself by putting her feelings into words until she was ready to hear information. Our own emotions can sometimes take over despite our best of intentions, and then we must forgive ourselves and start again.

Earlier in this chapter, I pointed out that most of us have become experts at the fight or flight skills which employ the power struggle responses and the responsibility/communication blockers. All are effective skills for *escalating* a power struggle: nagging, ordering, threatening, moralizing, using sarcasm, criticizing/judging what the other says or how he's acting, giving advice/telling the other what he "should" do. They all fit neatly into a position of the Drama Triangle.

The flight skills, believe it or not, also escalate a power struggle. In the attempt to *avoid* an issue altogether (Rescue position), the parent modeling any of the following three familiar responsibility-blockers is promoting the buildup of negative feelings:

Statement	Example
Reassuring	"Everyone says things they don't mean. I'm sure she's still your friend."
Distracting	"Come on, let's play a little soccer and you'll forget all about it."
Peace making	"It's okay. Go along with what your little sisters wants. After all, it's not easy being the youngest." *Or* "Let's not make a big deal out of this."

Each of these statements is an attempt to Rescue our child from feeling bad about something and/or an attempt to keep peace. Whenever we try to prevent our children from experiencing their emotions, we invite them to take a position and play the game.

Once we Rescue, we have encouraged our child to take the Victim position but remember what we've said about how people feel in this position. They don't like it and eventually jump up to Persecutor position. Once an overload of negative feelings has built up, the usual reaction is to blow up (Persecutor) over a seemingly little issue, and "voila" the game is in full swing.

Yes, we feel sad when our children are hurting, and we want to make the hurt go away. The fact is, we cannot make the hurt go away. Remember Chapter IV and the father whose son didn't make the A Team? We can only model a process for our children to recognize their feelings (don't forget to put those feelings into words) and move beyond the disappointment and negative feelings in a healthy way.

Whenever *we*, instead, take a position in the Drama Triangle, we invite our children to step in and play the game as we model how to play. Whenever parents and children play the game, the parents' goal is making their child "do as we say;" and the child's goal is "getting my parents off my back." No one is carrying out their rightful responsibility; and therefore, no one is addressing the actual problem.

Whenever we engage our children in the problem-solving process for resolving conflict, we are teaching them valuable skills necessary for learning how to take responsibility for their feelings and their choices and then to work toward solving the conflict rather than trying to win a game that can't be won.

As we step out of the Power Struggle ourselves, our children do gradually follow even if at first, kicking and screaming! As they learn responsibility and relationship-building skills, they become better and better at problem-solving. Through our consistent modeling and engaging our children in the process, they learn the skills for becoming responsible to themselves and to others. They learn that the most important goal in a conflict is reaching a mutually satisfactory solution and that the purpose for rules at home, in a job, on the road, is to ensure that everyone's needs are met.

Parenting is the most difficult job we'll probably *ever* do. And it's the most important job we'll *ever* have.

Reference List

Baumrind, Diane. 1967, 1971 Current patterns of parental authority. *Developmental Psychology*, 4(1, Pt2), 1-103
https://psycnet.apa.org/doi/10.1037/h0030372

Faber, Adele & Mazlish, Elaine. (1980). How to Talk So Kids Will Listen and Listen So Kids Will Talk. New York, NY: Avon Books, Inc.

Faber, Adele & Mazlish, Elaine. (1995). How to Talk So Kids Can Learn at Home and in School. New York, NY: Rawson Associates.

Glasser, W. (1975). Reality Therapy. New York, NY: Harper and Row.

Glasser, W. (2010). Choice Theory: A new Psychology of Personal Freedom. New York, New York. HarperCollins.

Gordon, T. (1975). Parent Effectiveness Training: The Tested New Way to Raise Responsible Children. New York, NY: Peter H. Wyden, Inc.

Gordon, T. (1989). Teaching Children Self Discipline at Home and at School. New York, NY: Times Books, Random House.

Holmes, J. H. (1984). "We Can Teach Students to Be Responsible." Phi Delta Kappa, 66, 50-52.

Karpman, Stephen (2014). A Game Free Life: The Definitive Book on the Drama Triangle and Compassion Triangle by the originator and author. (S.F. CA): Drama Triangle Publications.

ABOUT THE AUTHOR

Growing up, I was the "big sister," and helped raise my three much younger siblings. When I married at age nineteen, I knew just how to raise children-or so I thought.

So, when, by the age of twenty-four, I had three daughters of my own, all under three and a half, I felt confident in my parenting skills. My husband was all about rules and holding children to those rules. I too believed in being strict, but I was more laid back about the carry through.

I was completing my undergraduate work when our youngest entered Kindergarten and I started teaching secondary English. I knew little about interpersonal skills and believed a strict teacher was a strong teacher. Needless to say, I was a Boss teacher as I mentioned in the book. Then, two years later, when I enrolled in a Masters' Program in School Counseling, I was introduced to an alternative model for teaching *and* parenting–leader and guide instead of boss–also called the "Authoritative" Parent.

That was the beginning of my journey from teacher to school counselor and eventually to earning a doctorate in professional development–all professions requiring strong interpersonal skills. And parenting requires strong interpersonal skills. Parenting is all about creating nourishing and loving ways to interact with our children and adolescents while still holding them accountable for their behavior.

Based on my personal experience, as well as on the research, I can say emphatically that the ongoing results of becoming a lead parent are worth the struggles. AND witnessing the results two generations later in our own family, is truly one of the most rewarding experiences of my life.

My heart's passion is to share this process with others so that together, we might contribute to populating the world with compassionate, considerate, respectful, and responsible human beings!

I hope you have enjoyed this book and found it helpful in your life. If you are so inclined, please post a review at your favorite book site. Visit me at my website or drop me an email and let me know how you've been able to use any of the process to foster peace and respect in your life.

Good luck and please remember–never give up!

Judy Harmon Holmes

Author Contact Information
Email address: Dr.J@responsiblekids.org
Website: https://CreatingResponsibleKids.com
Facebook: Creating Responsible Kids

Publisher Contact Information
WC Publishing, an On-Target Words imprint
Info@OnTargetWords.com
147 Patriot Lane
Elkton, Florida 32033-4058 USA

ENDNOTES

[1] William Glasser, The Quality School (NY: Harper Collins, 1998), p 32 -36.
[2] Glasser, The Quality School, pp 25 – 32.
[3] Diana Baumrind, "The Influence of Parenting Style on Adolescent Competence and Substance Use. Journal of Early Adolescence 11 (1): 56-95, p 72.
[4] U.S. Department of Educations' National Center for Education Statistics, 2012.
[5] Thomas Gordon Parent Effectiveness Training (NY: Harmony House, 2019) pp 49-52.
[6] Adele Faber and Elaine Mazlish, How to Talk So Kids Will Listen $ Listen So Kids Will Talk (NY: Scribner, 2012) pp 1-47.
[7] Mary Budd Rowe, "Wait Time: Slowing Down May Be A Way of Speeding Up" Journal of Teacher Education, 1986. 37. (1):43-50
[8] Gordon, p 127.
[9] Thomas Gordon, p. 127
[10] https://www.monash.edu/news/articles/children-more-distracting-than-mobile-phones
[11] Faber & Mazlish, pp308-309 (and entire chapter on alternatives to punishment)
[12] Faber & Mazlish, pp 180 – 190.
[13] Gordon, p 51-52
[14] Stephen Karpman, A Game Free Life: The Definitive Book on the Drama Triangle and Compassion Triangle by the originator and author. (S.F. CA): Drama Triangle Publications. 2014.

www.ingramcontent.com/pod-product-compliance
Lightning Source LLC
LaVergne TN
LVHW051601070426
835507LV00021B/2707